WALKING THE BRIDGE

WITH A FEARLESS HEART

WALKING THE BRIDGE

WITH A FEARLESS HEART
Guidance from a Wisdom School Vol. 1

Diane Langlois Stallings

Walking the Bridge: With a Fearless Heart Guidance from a Wisdom School Vol. 1

Copyright © 2008 2009 2017 2019 by Diane Langlois Stallings
All rights reserved.

For information:
https://walkingthebridgewisdom.wordpress.com

ISBN: 978-0-9996411-0-1

Printed in the United States of America

10 9 8 7 6 5 4 3 2

Also in this series:
Walking The Bridge: With Balance - Vol. 2
Walking The Bridge: The Art of All-Is-Well - Vol. 3
Walking The Bridge: With Courage And Trust - Vol. 4

to Isaac

to our eternally dancing circle of friends

to all the fellowship in this earthly chariot

Contents

Why this Book? An Inner Journey	1
1 Mind Prism/ Source Flows into Specific Colors	5
2 Free Will/ Multi-storied Building Views/ Attachment	10
3 World is Made of Wisdom/ Light even within Dark	14
4 Being Present Now/ God is Everything	19
5 Sacred Song Brings Love/ Full Attention Brings Love	22
6 Find Joy/ Find God in the Ordinary	25
7 Dissonant World/ Narrow View, Broad View/ Big Mind	28
8 How to Deepen Prayer	31
9 Breath, Doorway to the Divine/ Alternate Nostril Breath	33
10 Paradox of the Now, No Time/ Dissolve into Unity	36
11 Control Appetites/ Horse, Rider/ Earthly Soul, Divine Soul	40
12 Subdue the Ego/ Deep Acceptance	43
13 Trust in God/ Baal Shem Tov	46
14 Pop into Divine Connection	50
15 A Story of Karma/ A Story of Healing	53
16 Ribnitzer Rebbe Releases a Lost Soul/ Deep Listening	56
17 In the Beam of God's Loving Attention	58
18 Ribnitzer Rebbe/ Hearing Torah	61

19 Pond of Ripples, Pond of Stillness	64
20 "I am" Meditation Practice/ Inner Witness	66
21 Bliss Orbit Meditation Practice/ Just Be	68
22 Your Life Purpose/ Four Archangels, a Bedtime Practice	71
23 Swami Rama/ Be the Witness/ There's Nothing Wrong	74
24 We are a Bottle in the Divine Ocean/ Inner Witness	77
25 Blessings and Curses/ God infuses All/ God is One	79
26 Ayin-Nothing and Yesh-Something	84
27 Maggid of Mezritch/ The First-day Light of God	87
28 Be the Divine Ocean	91
29 Elul / Returning	94
30 Ladder of Worlds/ Divine Pipeline/ Ego Separates Us	96
31 Stand Together/ Multi-level Skyscraper of Consciousness	99
32 Sukkot - Lose Yourself in Joy	104
33 Ribnitzer Rebbe/ Adam's World/ Go Vertical on Shabbos	107
34 Handling a Trigger/ Paying what's Due	111
35 World of Vibration/ Go Inward to Your Core	114
36 Rabbi Aryeh/ Deep Safety	117
37 Duality and Lack/ Abraham, Isaac, Jacob	120
38 Stop Efforting, Bask in the Sun/ Meditate on the Crown	122
39 Rabbi Baba Sali/ Humility	124
40 Servant of God, Child of God	126
41 Grace vs. Efforting/ Manna from Heaven	128
42 First Night of Hanukkah	130
43 Elisha/ Baba Sali/ Empty Your Vessel	133
44 You Are Never Alone/ Divine Help in Three Stories	135

45 Pipeline to All Worlds/ Align Thought, Speech, Action   139
46 Narrow View, Broad View   141
47 Something about the Sefirot   144
48 Carry Happiness Within/ Dispel Your Clouds   146
49 Freedom/ See Beyond Unconscious Behavior/ Marriage   150
50 Created New Every Moment/ Horizontal and Vertical   154
51 Right Brain/ Wordless Wisdom/ Discernment   156
52 Build Spiritual Energy/ Become the Divine Flute   161
53 Suffering and Equanimity   164
54 Purim/ Everything Arises Now   167
55 Choppy Waves/ "I'm sorry, I love you"/ You are Non-local   170
56 Golden Calf/ Errors/ Astral World/ Giving of the Torah   176
57 Stillness/ Wave-life and Still-life   181
58 Divine Mother/ Passover/ Increased Awareness   183
59 Holy of Holies, The Temple/ New Era/ Unusual Questions   188
60 Meditate on a Clear Pond/ Untie the Knot/ Handle Anger   196
61 Develop Awareness in Waking, Dreaming, Deep Sleep   200
62 Bottles in Bottles of Awareness/ Levels of Soul/ Time   205
63 Find God's Delight Inside/ Stand in Gratitude   209
64 Tainted Grain/ Tricky Ego/ Humility is Contentment   212
65 Livelihood/ God is Abundant   215
66 White Light, All Vibrations, Prism to Colors/ Swami Rama   217
67 Rosh Hashanah – New Year   221
68 Light in All Things/ World Made of Wisdom/ Atzilut   224
69 Sukkot/ Simcha Joy/ Amalek, Doubt and Trust   227
70 Lech Lecha, Release/ The Horizontal and The Vertical   230

71 Stay Out of the Story/ Gaze at God/ Av Harachaman	234
72 Tiferet, Balance of Strength and Loving-kindness	239
73 Connection/ Light Above Clouds/ Return the Gaze	243
74 Walk a Higher Level/ Patriarchs' Attributes/ Larger Self	247
75 Hanukkah/ Chochmah, Wisdom	253
76 Paradox/ Your Large Soul View/ Karma/ Kindness	256
77 Expansion, Evaporation Is True Prayer/ Gratitude	261
Appendix Tree of Life, Sefirot, Four Worlds	269
Encapsulations of Many of Isaac's Teachings	271
Index - Glossary	275
Acknowledgements	277
About the Author	280

WALKING THE BRIDGE

WITH A FEARLESS HEART

Why this Book? An Inner Journey

You and I walk this bridge, this tightrope across our troubled world and into the next world. It is frightening. This book answers fear with calm, with trust, with confidence that each step, no matter how it looks, is ultimately for the good.

You can release worry, strife, pain, and illusion.

Ever-increasing lightheartedness drew our community to listen to Isaac, whose words turned our egos upside down and transformed us. He took us from narrow view to broad view, where we accepted our shadows with humility and found strength. From light and dark, duality, we moved to wholeness, unity. We sailed together into higher perspective, into benevolent peace, into fields of speechless all-encompassing love.

In that Place all questions dissolved.

Total contentment.

In love with what-is.

But questions have a way of returning.

Why are we here? Why is there so much suffering in the world? How can I find my way? What is the greater reality beyond my small mind?

Isaac, our Rebbe, Torah scholar, enthusiast of many spiritual traditions, offered insights. A Rebbe is a teacher, but he insisted he was not a teacher, just another one of us on the path. (Isaac is a pseudonym - he prefers anonymity.)

Raised in the USA, Isaac trained many years in a Jerusalem yeshiva and became a rabbi. He later expanded his resources to include sages from India and other parts of the world. Our conversations explored Torah teachings, Tree of Life, Hasidism, mysticism, psychology, science, rabbis and gurus, sages and saints.

Isaac had an uncanny way of reaching right into our core. Each of us felt he spoke directly to our life, to our own issue-of-the-week.

The first time I ever heard him, a crack of vulnerability opened up. Uh-oh. A crack of honesty with my deepest self. A crack I could not un-see. Oh, no. This would be real work. This would disturb my life. This was a doorway to real transformation.

I could no longer hide from my true Self.

Isaac probed us to study our own hearts: "Try it out and see for yourself. Is this true for you?"

Meditation class began with music and singing. Isaac played his guitar, often joined by percussion and flute. Sacred songs composed by Isaac lightened up the atmosphere. After a silent meditation and more music, higher energies filled us. Then it was time to talk.

Isaac answered each question from the tone and spirit in which it was asked. The answer might be practical or mystical.

At those mystical times all of us, led by him, shifted into an expanded altered state. We went to a well of wisdom, a place of inclusion, ease, comfort, where everything made perfect sense. Nothing was wrong. We were Home.

When we returned to our ordinary awareness, we knew we'd enjoyed a delicious meal, but we often couldn't remember exactly what we'd tasted. This food for the soul nourished us in seen and unseen ways.

These conversations went beyond the brain, but my brain clamored to write them down, from memory, after each gathering. It was impossible to capture them truly in their fullness. My notes were unavoidably colored by my perception.

These pages are only what I heard through my own filters. They are paraphrased, so quotes are used sparingly.

Some topics arise more than once. The better to digest them. We often peel into new layers of awareness. We often hear the same message later in a brand new way. May it speak to your heart.

Whatever unfurled in our discussions, the theme always returned to cosmic love. A benevolent universe. It is in this spirit that these readings come to you. That no matter what is happening in your life, you may sense the One, the Source-of-all, holding you in Love.

- Diane Langlois Stallings

1 Mind Prism/ Source Flows into Specific Colors

Isaac said, "The mind is like a prism."

White light goes into the prism and is divided into many colors. The mind, the prism, separates and defines whatever it looks upon. It applies limits. Here's this particular color, it says. Different and separate from that particular color.

The world of no-mind is different than our ordinary world. It is vast, unlimited, undefined. It can't be understood by the mind.

The mind speaks only in color-language about specific colors.

Yet all colors come from the white light. The white light creates the colors.

So we live in a rainbow world that has limitations, compared to its unbounded origin in white light. The rainbow world gives rise to efforting. We might say, I have too much blue, I need more red. We struggle to get what we want. We overdo it and try to correct back to our first color. We try to keep one foot in each color.

But if we invite white light, the Divine, into our life, then our needs are filled and all colors automatically flow in wherever they belong. The best healing takes place this way. Our small mind doesn't know exactly what we need. We cannot fathom the Big Picture.

Many holy rebbes had the experience that when a person approached on the road for a consultation, that person's higher soul would go ahead of their body to have the first conversation with the rebbe, to clarify the root problem.

When the person arrived at the door and started talking in circles, "I want this to happen and then this," the rebbe already knew and had prayed for the deeper issue. He would suggest an odd remedy that was beyond that person's understanding.

The greatest blessing of all is the blessing for peace. Instead of asking for health, money, and all the things we think we need, peace fulfills us completely. It's like white light. If we have peace, we have everything.

Peace means we have reached our destination. In a position of peace, we have no more desire or fear.

Peace is timeless. It is only right now.

Desire and fear create our perception of time.

It takes so long for our desire to be fulfilled. We're waiting for it.

Fear puts pressure into time, making time shorter or longer.

Question: Tell us about free will.

In the rainbow world we seem to have free will. We make choices, we run our life, and we must take action. You can't stay home from work and ignore your obligations. At the same time, the World of White Light constantly feeds into this world and truly runs everything. Someday our higher self sees that we really had no choice, no free will. We did what God needed us to do. We are extensions of the divine presence.

The free will issue is a paradox, because on this plane we do have it, yet from a higher perspective we don't.

Here we seem to have choices. While we're living in this rainbow world, we must make good use of our choices.

In our tradition we have two ways of prayer that bring about change.

One is where you partner with God. You invoke God as a partner, and ask Him to bring in what you need.

Next comes the question, what kind of a partner have you been? Are you worthy of your divine Partner? How have you held up your end of the partnership? Are you pure enough? Real purity is pure and rare.

The second and less common way of prayer is to become nothing so God can come through you.

The Rebnitzer Rebbe, whom Isaac met, had chosen this path of humility so extreme that he became nothing. He actually looked scary, because you saw in his eyes, there was "nobody home." But really it's scary because of Who is there -- the immense Divine coming through his eyes.

In fact he said a blessing over a blind infant, who had been born without all the parts in the eyes to see. The doctors said the child would never see. After their visit to the Rebnitzer Rebbe, the parents brought the baby back to the doctors. Lo and behold, the missing parts were there, and the child was no longer blind. Inexplicable.

For meditation we need to remember that behind all the noise of the mind there's a continuous peace. Your higher soul is always in touch with it, no matter what happens here. Your higher soul stays in contentment.

Even in a crisis, you may feel a deep calmness that everything is okay.

Question: Isaac, please say a few words about dreams and deceased loved ones coming to us in our dreams.

Our imagination can inflate and convince us of things that aren't necessarily true. We must be careful and discerning. Do not believe everything that arises. And yet there are times when our loved ones are saying hello. Sometimes we won't feel the accuracy of this until later. Truth may resonate in deeper layers as time goes by.

Virtually nobody's intuition is 100% reliable.

Don't put any stock in psychics and people who claim to have "the real story" on anything. If a psychic is accurate half the time, we tend to believe they are accurate all the time. But this is not so.

In the ancient world, if a prophet was wrong just one time, they were deemed a false prophet. They were put to death for it.

Don't waste time listening to psychic suppositions.

Our time and attention is much better spent in learning compassion and stillness. Meditate a little longer.

Keep polishing your own cup, because that's the one thing you can do. We each have charge of our own cup, our own character development. We cannot predict when God will pour blessings into our cup. God's gifts to us are gifts, not foreseeable to us.

If your cup is leaky, in disrepair, it will not hold anything. You won't even notice when grace pours into you and slips away.

Whether your cup receives anything or not, you can polish it, check it for leaks, put it back on the table in hopes of receiving. Give your attention to your own purity of heart and mind.

2 Free Will/ Multi-storied Building Views/ Attachment

To begin each meeting, Isaac always played guitar. Our singing expanded our hearts, released our cares, lifted our joy. After a silent meditation, we'd have more music and song. Then our discussion.

Question: I wonder if I actually have any free will? When I make healthy choices about food or exercise, maybe it's Divine Will, not my own, so what's the point of choosing?

Think of a tall building, many stories tall, a skyscraper. You live on a particular floor, and your friend may live on another. From each floor of this building, the views are unique. The views change, depending what floor you're standing on.

The people of each level have their own shared view of reality.

We who are living on the lower levels think we have free will, and in effect we do. That's how it looks on the first floor.

On the first floor, from your window you see people walking by, dogs, trucks and taxis.

Higher up, you see only clouds and birds. Angels are so high up in the multi-storied building, they have no free will. They have the bigger perspective that shows how everything is God's will. They do only the will of God. They're unable to do anything else.

In the same way, when an evolved saint does what we consider a miracle, it's only because he or she is aligned with the Divine Will.

Are your healthy choices from your own free will? Yes, when seen from some floors of the building. From the upper floors whatever unfolds is Divine Will.

Eventually we are meant to rise higher in this multi-storied building. We are meant to gain awareness and a broad view. It's no accident that life is tough on the first floor of the building. You have dirt, trash, noise, even violence in the street. On the first floor, we have more suffering.

Suffering is meant to loosen our grasp on our attachments.

Can we become conscious within our suffering? Can we give it a closer look? Can we be more aware of what is happening when we suffer?

People tend to be half-asleep, plowing through, fighting back, believing it's a dog-eat-dog world, and the best defense is to attack other dogs.

Eventually it may dawn on us that we ourselves cause our own suffering.

We hold firm expectations that don't get filled.

We hold rigid behaviors.

We hold the desires and fears of this world, this level.

We hold attachments. With enough suffering, we might begin to see how our attachments make us hurt.

We may spend lifetimes, eons, on that first floor of suffering, choosing, efforting, holding so many attachments in so many ways. Not conscious, not aware.

Through the grace of God we gain more awareness and find ourselves on the second floor. But the second floor has a different style of attachments.

As God pulls you up through the floors, you let go of attachment to the things of each floor. You might do it with great difficulty, screaming about it, or you might do it with ease.

Whatever we think is outside of us, is really inside of us.

God works through us. No one else has your particular abilities or perspective. Each person is vital to the whole puzzle.

The whole reason for creation is this: We separate from God, into duality, for the joy of reuniting someday.

Wisdom is available to learn every day, not just at the end of life.

Sages would ask, if today were your last day on earth, where does it hurt? Where do you feel the pain of letting go of this world? What are you attached to?

Question: What's the difference between love and attachment in relationships?

Love is unconditional giving.

Attachment is doing business. Such as, "I'll give you this, you give me that." It is business even if it's done very generously: "I'll give you two, you give me one." That's still expectation. Attachment to outcome.

Question: Are we designed to partner?

Some may see it that way. But the soul is whole unto itself - complete in itself. The bottom line is, you don't need a soulmate in order to be whole. You're already whole.

No doubt a partner can help you grow. Often through conflict. Partnership is good sandpaper for the ego. It trims your rough edges and softens your ego.

Either way, with a partner or without, we want to find our attachments.

The best way to find your attachments is to meditate daily. This strengthens your Inner Witness and helps you see yourself more clearly. Over time you'll gain a more broad view.

Here's our best advice. You need to remember only two things:

God is everywhere in everything, and

Everything is for the Good.

Question: God goes with me even when I do things that aren't right?

Yes - the Baal Shem's teaching is that the Shekhinah, the Divine Presence, goes with you every moment. When you do small-minded actions, She weeps for Her exile. That is, your attitude shuts Her out from your awareness. Yet She is with you always.

So at the point of temptation, remember, you bring God everywhere.

3 World is Made of Wisdom/ Light even within Dark

No matter how many times our mind wanders in meditation, if we can keep bringing it back, we've done a good job. "Shuv" means return. The Sages say the one who returns again and again despite distraction is considered higher than the tzaddik (saint).

Question: What can we do when we feel such a yearning for God, but we can't find a clear connection? Sometimes I taste great sweetness in meditation, and sometimes nothing.

We need to recognize our very yearning is God's touch upon us. The fact that we yearn means the divine connection is already there. God has made contact, touching us with yearning, to bring us to Him.

Question: The more I meditate, the more I enjoy it. In fact everything else pales in comparison. I'd rather come to meditation group than go to the movies with family and friends. They see that I no longer enjoy the things they enjoy, and there's discomfort in that. In a sense I'm slipping away from them. We don't fully share as much as we used to.

Look, said Isaac. You have a table filled with marbles. You consider that some marbles are yours. Those other marbles are not yours. You have a band to go around your own marbles. A boundary. You consider these marbles to be yourself. This is me. Those out there - all that stuff is not me. I have my own bundle of marbles.

But the further we evolve, the more we realize that this odd marble is also me. And so is the next one. We expand our borders. We stretch and expand the band around the marbles until we contain them all.

I am not only myself. I discover I am you. I am the tree. I am the wind.

Isaac quoted the Torah, "God made everything with wisdom." This is read in two ways. Not only did God use His wisdom to create the world, but the world is literally composed of the substance of wisdom, Chochmah.

Even the densest physical things have the attribute of wisdom in them. It's what they are made of. Some are more covered up than others. When we have the eyes to see it, to uncover it, we find wisdom in everything. God in everything. Nothing is boring. Nothing is less desirable than anything else.

The expansion of wisdom is the whole point of this world's existence.

This is the ground from which all being arises. Each and every thing is made of wisdom.

The wisdom is revealed when all the pieces of the puzzle are put together and you have a picture you didn't have before. Every bit of it plays its part.

Question: I can envelop lots of things, but I can't find a place in my heart for war. What do we do with the really horrible stuff?

Isaac held up his hand like a claw and said sometimes a puzzle piece is extremely dense and has very hard edges. Its boundaries are so tight. It knows what it is, and it is not like anything else. When a piece is like this, it is more ego-bound than anything else.

When I believe I am my own shape, I am deepest into my ego. I know where my edge is, and I stop there.

But when the puzzle piece is put into the whole puzzle and finds its unique spot, its edges disappear. You no longer see the borders of each piece. You see the beautiful picture they all make together.

Sometimes you'll see God revealed in places we consider too negative.

The Sages say the highest light is actually hidden in the deepest matter. The most dense dark aspects of our world actually hold the most light, if we could uncover them. Someday matter itself will be the Light.

Ramalinga Swami, who lived in the 1800's, prayed to be given a perfect body. To us that may sound unspiritual, but that was his prayer. His body grew so healthy, going beyond ordinary health. As he went through the stages of it all, he wrote 40,000 verses, a very long poem, recording the entire experience.

His body became golden in hue. The skin glowed with a golden light. You could see light escaping from the skin. He called this the "golden body." Soon it was impervious to any illness or injury. They couldn't drown it or set it on fire. They shot bullets that didn't penetrate him.

Then he advanced to the "body of grace." At that point he saw blessings everywhere he turned. Beauty almost too great to bear. When he took a breath, every breath was so sweet it would make him swoon.

Eventually his body didn't even cast a shadow. Some of his followers were frightened by this, so he made sure to wear his turban and cloak. That way the clothes cast a shadow, and people weren't so scared of him.

God then asked him if he would like to wear the body of the Universe. He said yes. One day he vanished right in front of his disciples. There was a flash of purple light, and he disappeared.

From this we can see that both the body and the soul manifest God. It's just that most of our bodies are hiding God, or we think they are, more than our soul hides God.

Mitzvot, good deeds, are designed to bring the light out, to bring God out of hiding.

The more lightness, the higher the vibration. When you feel good about everything, light-hearted, your vibration is a higher frequency. In meditation, we release all concerns and hopefully move toward a lighter tone inside, a higher vibration.

Ancient yogis would spend 10,000 years perfecting a particular technique in order to reach a certain vibration. But that same vibration arises spontaneously when one weeps tears of love for God.

These vibrations are contagious, from person to person, from candle to candle, lighting up our hearts.

Can we now, in the Present Moment, relax and open to the idea that nothing is wrong? Young children seem to do this easily. Perhaps you can remember a time when you were very young, and it was a rainy day, and school was cancelled. Suddenly the whole day stretched out with endless possibilities. But right now you are in the joy of the rain, in the joy of this moment of newfound freedom. Nothing matters but your young and happy heart. Everything is fresh in this moment.

When you are fully present, everything is fresh bread. Why would you ever want day-old bread, the stuff that is not right here right now?

4 Being Present Now/ God is Everything

Question: I need a tool to learn to be present. The past is gone and the future is a fantasy. Only now is real. I can get to the now, but there's nothing to hang onto there, and my thoughts flood in. It reminds me about the way God put Moses into a crack in the rock so he could "see" God. I know that crack is the Now.

Yes, God said to Moses, "I will cover and protect you. I will pass and you will see Me from behind."

Elokim (Elohim) is the word for God of the past and the future, of duality.

The crack is Now. That's the only place we find Havayah (God's Essence, God Presence).

Usually the sun of God's light is shielded by clouds. A little crack opens up between clouds, and light pours forth. But finding God in that crack is always a Gift. All we can do is make our cup ready and hope that it is filled by God. We may wait forever, but it is worth it.

Yearning indicates separateness, and when we feel separate, this leads to the first awareness of God. So yearning is God's first touch on us.

In the parsha (scripture passage) where God asks Moses to confront Pharaoh, He says, "Come to Pharaoh" which means, "and I'll be waiting there for you. Come here." God is there with Pharaoh, waiting for Moses to arrive with his request.

"And Pharaoh will say no, and you ask again, 'Let my people go.'"

This is the parsha used by every rebbe to teach about free will. Because, doesn't it look like God is holding two puppets here?

God had to talk him into it. Moses didn't want to go. God says, "Come here, and Pharaoh will say no, and you say again, let my people go, and he says no, and then come here again and Pharaoh will say no - -."

When it comes down to it, even though we think we are running our lives, we are God's puppets, fulfilling what is needed. And God loves his puppets.

Question: So does this mean predestination?

That's not the point, exactly.

We are all one. God is One. That's what we say, our highest prayer. God is One. So there can't be free will.

Wherever there are two or more, in duality, there's the appearance of free will, and the appearance of separateness.

But all the time, we are One. Not separate. God is One.

It's important to know and remember that the Unity, the Oneness, the Witness doesn't look with a cold scientific eye. No, the Witness loves all it sees. You can feel this in meditation. This sense of comfort, of love.

Keter (the crown) is the quality of unconditional love. This is the place we hope to access through meditation.

It is fine to be wherever you are in the sefirot at any time. Even a feeling of revenge is part of Gevurah. Aggression is Netzach. (Some of the ten attributes known as sefirot include "Chesed" Loving-kindness at the right arm, "Gevurah" Discipline at the left arm, "Tiferet" Harmony balanced between them. "Netzach" Assertion at the right hip, "Hod" Surrender at the left hip.)

When and if you are aligned with Keter, then every response is fully appropriate to the moment. You are soft when needed and strong when needed. The correct energy flows to the correct channel. This is the position of the Witness.

Let's say you have a child, and you told them not to touch this thing, and they did, and they broke it, and you're angry. Your other child walks in to show you a picture they drew and you are fuming so much you just say "That's nice" – but you're still back in the anger with the first child. You're not in Keter. You're further down in the sefirot.

God wants to play us like a flute. God wants to play us new in each moment. But our keys get stuck. We're stuck on the first incident. Stuck on the way it grabs us.

God wants to play us, play music through us, if we can be clear enough.

The Sages say a person is like a coal. A coal may be dark and inert, but it's always hot. When God blows on it, it becomes fire.

Meditation is not escape. It's diving. Everything is God, from the top of the busy wave to the depths of the sea. When you dive to the depths, you are deeper than all your joys and sorrows. But this is not escape. It's the deeper view of All-That-Is.

5 Sacred Song Brings Love/ Full Attention Brings Love

Question: Please give us your teaching on song and evaporation?

Okay, first let me tell you about two rebbes who were brothers - Elimelekh and Zusya. Elimelekh felt that the easiest path to the divine was through discipline and making oneself humble. Zusya felt that the path was through love and the flame of passion for God.

They took their question to their teacher, the Maggid of Mezritch, Dov Baer.

He said, you are both right. Both are good paths.

It's good to take the way of Gevurah, of discipline. I sit and pray because it's time to do that; I make myself nothing before God, I am nothing in the vast scheme. But also the way of Chesed, of love and song, expands us to the same degree that a thousand years of prayer might do.

The act of singing a spiritual song generates flames of love in the heart. This heat causes the mind and the ego to evaporate, up into the clouds. Then the divine clouds rain down upon us.

After singing a song together, we notice that in the silence afterward, we feel Heaven's response to us. A palpable bliss descends upon us. Many in this group can feel it.

Bliss rains down on us. Yet we can't make it happen. It is always a gift to us.

Question: Please comment on the current "Shift" that's supposed to be happening for humanity?

Everybody wants the big answer that will solve everything. You won't find it on a distant mountaintop or in the mystical books locked away in vaults. All I can do in my life is to lay each brick straight, so the wall won't be crooked as the years go by.

All you need to do is give your full attention to whatever is in front of you right now. I listen and speak with lots of people, and I find that as I give my attention, love arises.

It is your attention that causes love to arise. That lofty idea, Love, which everyone constantly seeks, is right here available constantly. This ordinary world IS the divine manifestation. Take it in and respect it as Such.

We are our attention. Attention is the only thing we can give.

Everything else we think we have belongs to God, not to the "little me." The only thing "little me" can possibly offer is attention.

This is what our loved ones and children crave from us. Attention.

What happens in meditation or prayer, when we give our attention to God?

You know God is always gazing upon us, caring for us. The Sages say that if He forgot us for one moment, we would cease to exist.

So what happens when you grow calm enough to return that gaze?

Ahh . . .

"Bliss is the response of Eternity to the finite looking at It," said Isaac.

6 Find Joy/ Find God in the Ordinary

Question: How we can best prepare for Purim, the holiday of joy?

Begin to understand that this world around us is not what it seems to us. We so easily take it for granted that life is this way, or that way. We assume it's all predictable, that's just the way it is. We think God created the world eons ago, and here it is, sort of static.

No. It is not static. God creates the world new each moment. God is gazing upon us. God is infusing everything. There's a constant unfolding, a constant conversation here. It arises fresh and new each moment.

To move into joy, we need to see creation as an expression of God, in the moment. See all the ordinary things as coming to us from God.

We like to look for the extraordinary and say God is there. An amazing sunset. A newborn baby. A close shave on the highway, when we didn't crash. A remarkable synchronicity that resonates as a divine message to us.

Yet. We should learn to see God even in the ordinary.

In fact nothing is ordinary. There is no ordinary moment.

When we feel everything is ordinary and dull, we are asleep to the larger reality.

The small you isn't "you," because a huge part of you exists on the divine plane. The larger part of you looks upon the small you and loves it. The larger part of you is always at peace, always fully satisfied, always loving everything.

Can you, right now, in the expanded place after meditation, take a look and love every part of yourself?

All of us have, at some point, recognized that this is a dream world. Something uncanny, inexplicable, extraordinary, pops up. Things happen that science cannot explain. Synchronicities, we call them. When synchronicity hits, we can clearly see what a dream this world is. Divine intervention does happen, in ways large and small. Those are astonishing moments that wake us up within this dream.

But can you love the ordinary moment and see it as God? When you recognize God right here without any extraordinary influence, then you're truly learning.

Question: I've heard you say good deeds are a path to joy.

Yes, mitzvot - good deeds - are both a path toward and a natural expression of joy. There are different ways to do mitzvot. The most common is the "mitzvot-in-waiting," which is the attitude that I'll do this because I should do it, and it will give me spiritual wealth. Do it and get "rich."

But a true mitzvah happens when your joy overflows from you so much that you can't contain it. You feel compelled to share that joy.

Like with great music praising the One, the Hasids were so filled with joy, they had to get up and dance.

Some people, when they are filled with joy, tend to get very still and quiet. Some overflow their joy by nurturing others, giving, spreading the joy.

You don't have to push yourself through life. Don't force it. You can be in an allowing accepting space, where even the dog barking sounds like Eternity to you. You can love it as well as anything else.

Surrender to Love. Yes, within this moment now. Breathe.

You see? Bliss is always available, every moment. Always here.

7 Dissonant World/ Narrow View, Broad View/ Big Mind

Question: So much is wrong in the world. I don't want to accept and allow the bad stuff. You say it will bring me peace, but at what price?

The price is to give up narrow view in favor of broad view.

This world of duality always holds dark and light. We always have both. And we have our opinion of both. We cling to those opinions. We tell ourselves the dark should not be here. But it is an intrinsic part of the show. It's not going to leave.

What we really need is a bigger mind, a broad perspective.

Have you ever watched an ant hill, or maybe two ant hills in conflict? A lot is going on down there, right? But you have a broad view, and that scene is only one small part of your reality.

In meditation, we hopefully let go of opinions and find a tone of peace with everything. We go to "big mind," and we're able to take in everything, including the negative stuff, as part of the whole beautiful world.

Or imagine yourself coming into the theater of life, to watch stories take place on the screen. You're going to need darkness. The house lights have to be dim in order to see the movie. It's the darkness that puts you into the illusion of the story.

Within a short while, you feel yourself are inside the movie, don't you? Things are happening. Your heart is speeding up or slowing down, according to the story. It's all an illusion, but you buy into it. You're impacted by the darkness in the theater as well as the stress and drama of the story.

The darkness, the difficulty, has an important role in this earthly world.

Good music contains dissonance, and is richer because of that dissonance.

Here's a beautiful chord of many notes on the guitar - but now take only two of those many notes – B and C played right next to each other. They grate on the ear. They sound scary. Yet with the whole chord, beauty.

In the same way, the incense of the old temple held eleven fragrances, one of which was a stench by itself. You would never want to bring that into the temple. Yet when added to all the other smells, it produced fullness. It gave more body to the whole blend. It made the whole orchestra of fragrances complete.

In our own memories, we might see how some negativity in an event adds to the whole experience. Those are surely the best life stories we like to tell each other, aren't they? Life was so tough, look what we went through, but we made it.

See the Whole picture, instead of narrowing your vision down to one negative thing. The moment you focus on one thing, that's your doorway into time, into duality, into the loss of the panorama.

When you get hooked into narrow view, try to back up into broad view.

As with King David's psalm, "Shiviti Hashem l'negdi tamid" - "I place God before me always." You can see the name of God before you always. Each person is God. Can we fathom that?

"I see the name of God before me always." This was a practice from ancient times, and you can try it. Imagine the Hebrew name of God, the Yod-Hey-Vav-Hey, overlaying everything you look upon. Wherever you look, there It is. There is God.

8 How to Deepen Prayer

Question: About ego – it seems like it's my ego when I want to be right?

Yes, that's one aspect of the ego talking: "I'm right." It's the need to be right and correct. We see it easily in other people, and we tend to not see it in ourselves. In oneself it masquerades as correctness, having a good answer, helping others see the light, and such like that.

Question: How can I go deeper in prayer?

Concentration, which leads you into meditation, is a great adjunct to prayer, and it will take you deeper.

Try 20 or 30 minutes of watching the natural breath. This may feel boring, but it sharpens the mind's concentration. It will grow your patience.

As a culture, we are too impatient. Our minds too busy. We're over-stimulated. We turn on the TV for continued distraction. So when we first sit to concentrate and meditate, it feels too slow and boring. We're not accustomed to a state of peace. But we thrive in peace. It does require practice. It's a learned experience, to enjoy peace.

Another technique is to simply feel your crown, feel the top of your head, and stay aware of it continuously. This increases concentration.

After you have mastered concentration, then you begin to truly meditate. You hold awareness on a subject (yourself) and an object (your head, your breath, your chosen focal point). Here I am with the object of my attention. Subject and Object. Keep holding both. Eventually the two merge into one. You go into a unified state. Union. All is One.

Meditation brings a taste of positive divine delight. This is not negative delight, which is the removal of troubles. Positive delight is actually awareness of the Divine.

Your first response to it is, "Wow." The very verbalization of Wow puts you back into your logical wordy mind. At this point you are more attached to explaining, talking about, and describing the divine experience than in actually staying there to feel it. Maybe someday we'll get to the point where we will stay in the unified state longer.

But we cannot force it to happen. It is a gift to us. Divine Connection. It's important to remember you will never have control of it, never have charge of it.

In the unified state, subject and object become One. That means 'you' disappear, merge into the Oneness. It is deep surrender. There is no 'me' in that state. All is One.

9 Breath, Doorway to the Divine/ Alternate Nostril Breath

After a sweet silent meditation, everybody was speechless.

Isaac spoke about the two bodily systems that feed the entire body.

The first is the circulatory system, the heart and the bloodstream. As we know, the blood carries food and oxygen to every cell. The Sages spoke about toxicity of the blood, turbidity. This happens when our diet and exercise are poor, when our liver is overburdened with toxins, or when our negative emotions overrule us.

In fact Reb Nachman wrote a whole essay about the effect these emotions have on our blood system. When we are angry, our heart beats faster. There is in fact a different pattern of heartbeat for each emotion – for jealousy, for anxiety, sadness, depression.

We can associate the blood system with Nefesh, the physical level of our soul. Our life force vitality.

When our emotions, exercise, oxygenation, and diet are clean, then the circulatory system is in good form. Then we have access to become aware of the second system, the nervous system.

We all know the nervous system enervates every part of our body. Spiritual circles speak of this system actually feeding energy to the body. Sages in India are able to go without food, because all their energy comes in from Divine Source, through the nervous system, to fuel every physical cell of the body. They've been doing this for centuries.

When we get our blood in order, when blood and heart are healthy and calm, then we can begin to feel this energy in the nervous system.

The nervous system has two ways of working – autonomic and voluntary. That is, most of our organs run automatically. We don't tell the heart to beat or the stomach to digest. They do their jobs automatically without our conscious management of them.

But we do manage the voluntary muscles of our arms and legs. They operate when our brain tells them to do so.

The one part of the body that is both automatic and voluntary is our lungs. We can either allow the breath to come in without thinking about it, or we can control our breathing. Also, here in the lungs, we have the intersection of the circulatory system, the lowest physical part of us, with the nervous system, where the Divine enters the physical.

If we focus on breath and become conscious of it, we have a doorway to the Divine. All spiritual traditions throughout the world have taught us this.

In order for us to have access to this wonderful gateway, we must get our blood in order and our emotions calmed. As we use the breath in our meditation, we will tap into Divine energy. We may begin to feel a beautiful sensation in our body, or hear a beautiful divine sound, or see a beautiful brilliant light.

Sometimes that inner light looks so bright that when we stop meditating and open our eyes, the outer world dims by comparison. As if someone just dimmed the lights.

Alternate nostril breathing is a beginner's step in breath-control meditation. Place the thumb and ring finger upon either side of the nostrils. The first two fingers can rest on the forehead, on the 3rd eye. You will inhale through one nostril, then press it closed, retain the breath, exhale through the other nostril, and inhale again on that side.

Inhale to a count of 7. Hold the full breath for a count of 7. Exhale through opposite nostril for a count of 7. Inhale through that nostril, hold, and return breath out through the first nostril. Repeat and continue awhile. If the 7 count feels too long for you, adjust it. Enjoy the practice of this.

Beginning meditators may find the breath boring, but breath practice builds our patience and provides a true doorway to Divine Connection.

10 Paradox of the Now, No Time/ Dissolve into Unity

Rabbi Chaim Volozhin, in the late 1700's, was the number one student of Rabbi Elijah of Vilna, a brilliant man, a Talmudic scholar like no other. Elijah of Vilna was the leader of the traditionalists, who at that time excommunicated the Hasidim and their leader, the Baal Shem Tov.

Rabbi Elijah of Vilna had an astounding grasp of Torah as well as science, mathematics, astrology, all sorts of subjects. By the age of ten his knowledge surpassed his teachers, and at eleven he had memorized the entire Talmud. Even as a young man he was well known and respected for his wisdom. Professors would come to ask for his help on the question they'd been working on for years, and Rabbi Elijah would offhandedly give them the exact answer they needed.

His main student was Rabbi Chaim, and we can trust his interpretation of Torah.

Chaim says the main precept of our tradition and all monotheism is that God is One. Everything is God. Not only that, but God creates the world new every minute. There is no yesterday. We think there was, but there wasn't. There is no time. Only in our memories does time exist.

Chaim speaks of the Upper Yehidah, which means union with God, and the Lower Yehidah, the world of Malkhut where we live. In Malkhut we believe in progress, time, yesterday and tomorrow.

But the higher reality is: no time, everything arises right now, is created right now. Memory is the only thing that makes us believe in the past.

When we say our daily prayer, the Sh'ma, we proclaim that God is One. God is all that is. There is nothing but God.

The light of God is hidden in this world, yet all of it IS God.

We think we have a point of view – "I am Isaac" – but really that's an illusion. God is dreaming us. If the Dreamer stops dreaming or takes His attention away from anything, even for a moment, that thing would cease to exist.

God is dreaming us in every moment, recreating us.

God comes through us, all of us, and at the same time God is beyond us, dreaming us. Those few who rise to Unity with God – they disappear into Unity. They are no longer 'themselves' at all. They have no point of view while in Unity. When they return to our world, the world of Malkhut, they bring the fragrance of the divine with them.

Only those who can become nothing will reach Unity.

Abraham was nothing even though he was the leader of nations.

The Talmud speaks about 36 hidden tzaddikim (the "Lamed Vav," meaning 36), the unknown saints of every generation, deeply humble righteous ones who uphold the merit of humanity. By their practice and prayer, they avert disaster for all of us. These tzaddikim are constantly rising into the Upper Yehidah of Unity and bringing back that fragrance to the earth. The Shabbos (Sabbath) songs are all about that fragrance coming in.

Question: How would we recognize someone who is bringing in that fragrance?
They are so humble and so hidden, you wouldn't recognize them. The only clue might be that they are inexplicably happy, and they keep growing happier, for no apparent reason.

When God came to Moses in the burning bush, the literal translation of God's words is, "I will be what I will be." "Ehyeh Asher Ehyeh."
Moses asked God for His name, so he could tell the people. God said to tell them, "I will be what I will be." That's His name. Because God dreams each thing into existence.

Moses' opponent was Amalek, whose name means doubt. Amalek kept chasing Moses through the desert. Just as doubt chases us.
The Torah tells us, "You shall blot out the remembrance of Amalek from under heaven; you shall not forget it." Like, don't forget to blot out doubt.
In other words, "Remember to Forget." We need to forget our doubt, forget our memory, forget the past, forget ourselves. Dissolve into Unity.
When we meditate, we should not be in a position of waiting. Waiting for something to happen. Waiting for insight.
The paradox we hold is that all time is now. There is nothing to wait for.
Also the paradox is that we don't exist in the way we think. We are vessels for God. We are infinite people, "b'tzelem

Elohim" – created in the image of God. We are always filled with infinite worth.

Now. As the Buddhists say, even to hear this teaching without understanding is a deep blessing, which you may wait 10,000 years to receive.

11 Control Appetites/ Horse, Rider/ Earthly Soul, Divine Soul

Isaac told a story about the brothers, Rabbi Elimelech and Rabbi Zusya, whose communities supported them comfortably. But every so often they wanted to get back to humility. So they would travel as beggars, wearing rags, eating only whatever was given to them.

On one such occasion, in the middle of the icy Russian winter, they walked into an inn to warm themselves by the fire. The inhabitants were drinking and getting more joyful, starting to dance in a big circle. As the circle danced around, one dancing drunk thought it would be fun to hit Zusya in the shoulder as he went by. So every round, he whacked him. Zusya put up with it peaceably for awhile. Then he moved a bit further away, and the man reached further to hit him. Finally Eli, who had a much more reserved demeanor than Zusya, traded places with Zusya. And finally the punchy drunk stopped.

Aggression seems to be part of our animal nature in this rough world. Even in Nature programs you see how violent the animal world is. Eat or be eaten. The fish swim upstream in great peril. Only a few of them reach the top, spawn, and die.

They give their life for sex. Mate and die. Males have bright appendages to attract the females. In effect the males are saying 'look at me, I'm the best' and compete to be chosen. They fight each other for it. Females sit still and choose. Over and over again, this pattern plays out. It's a violent world. It's like high school, with all the competition and sex.

As a young child I enjoyed playing outdoors, and everything seemed harmonious. The frogs and snakes and insects were my friends. I would pet them, and they would stay in my hand.

When I started grade school, I saw people being cruel to each other. In high school the cruelty and violence were even more pronounced. I thought, if this is what life is, I'm going to be depressed forever.

But then I began to look at spiritual teachings of all kinds. At my yeshiva in Jerusalem, one of the primary teachings was in learning to control one's appetites. Not only food but anger, lust, jealousy, aggression. To control that urge the drunk felt to smack a beggar in the shoulder.

It's one thing to hear this and think you understand it, but it's a challenge to practice it. How difficult is it to control our appetites? We know it's anything but easy.

Nefesh Habehamit is the most earthly soul with earthly appetites. It's the horse. Your divine soul, Neshama, is the rider. You don't want your horse, your appetites, to ride you. We've all seen this happen, in others or in ourselves. A life ruled by appetite, impulse, excess.

You want to take charge and keep your divine soul in the saddle. Let the horse become a good servant to you. Not your master. You don't want to be a slave to your earthly appetites.

We could say, too, this horse is our ego. The ego is not a bad thing. We need it, so we can function here in practical ways. But if you want progress on your spiritual path, you can't leave the ego in charge.

We all have the challenge of riding our horse, of limiting our animalistic reactions.

When we control our appetites, it should be for spiritual reasons - that we want to get closer to God. Not that we want to keep our body healthy – although that's a good reason too.

We see a cupcake and say "oo." Our appetite is aroused. The desire for more kicks in. More sweets, more chocolate. Yet we also know this distraction pulls us away from divine connection. Maybe we could compromise, try half a cupcake, and offer the non-half as our effort toward the divine.

While we say "oo," give me more, another part of us says "Oy."

You want it and you don't. You know it's not good for you. But you should make the choice not because you want to look slimmer or be healthier. Rather, the curbing of appetite is a spiritual skill we want to develop.

We need both the horse and the rider. Neither should be discounted. In the Torah line that says, "You shall love the Lord with all your heart," the word 'heart' is spelled strangely. It has a double letter that shouldn't be there. The double letter indicates you are loving God with your body and soul. Both horse and rider.

12 Subdue the Ego/ Deep Acceptance

The soul must learn to control the ego, as a rider controls a horse. You restrain your desire; you choose to eat a half-cupcake. This is supernatural, because your natural inclination is to eat a whole cupcake or two.

When I lived in Jerusalem and spent time with the elderly rabbis, I found them to be so beautiful and inspiring. They had spent their whole lives engaged in controlling ego through their orthodox practices. Every time I visited them, I came away both inspired and depressed, for I knew I would never be able to subdue my ego habits to the degree they had done.

I couldn't hide my shortcomings. God and the higher realms see everything about us every moment. When it comes down to it, in the spiritual world we have no privacy. But we are loved and accepted, no matter what.

Rabbi Baba Sali worked hard his whole life to diminish every aspect of his ego – his anger, fear, jealousy, laziness. In his state of divine alignment, miracles arose. He demonstrated so clearly that the outer world is a reflection of our inner state.

Again and again in the Torah, God states, "I am your God." The deeper translation and meaning of this is, "I am your mirror." I am your personal God. I am what you project.

When you make this shift in your understanding, natural law falls away.

Isaac said he used to drink wine on sacred holidays. One time he had no money in the budget for it. He would have bought two bottles, and he really wanted them. But he gave it to God, saying something like, "If it's going to happen, You do it please." He went out to do the yard-work, whacking down his tall grass. On the first whack, there lay a twenty dollar bill, which at the time was just enough to buy two bottles of wine.

Another time when he was immersed in reading the scriptures, he became so blissed-out, he wondered if the divine connection was real. He wondered if it was just his own mind, convincing him to feel such bliss. So he asked for a sign. Such chutzpah, he had then. He said, "God, if these feelings of bliss are authentic, coming from You, then please make a bird fly into my room." Not an outrageous idea, because birds liked to visit his balcony and eat the bird seed. No bird came in that day. Hmm. But the next day, during his studies, a bird flew to him and hovered right in front of his face with full eye contact for 30 seconds. What a message.

We think life is ordinary. Nothing is new. But life arises new in each moment.

Some people wouldn't know paradise if it landed right on top of them. No matter what we are given, no matter how wonderful life is, we keep seeking to improve it. We say, it's nice, but it would be even better if we could move this tree a few feet over, or move these flowers. We always want to improve it.

So we dismiss paradise.

By the same token, we wait for a 'good experience' in meditation. As long as you're waiting, it cannot arrive, because you are in waiting mode. Not appreciating mode.

When we learn to really enjoy what's already here, then we're on the right track.

We cannot get this by reading books. We're seeking a way to BE. We're seeking to appreciate what is here, now, in front of us.

Have you ever been in that state of deep acceptance with everything, and you feel intoxicatingly happy? You look around, and no matter what's going on, you can hold all the events of your day, all the ups and downs. All of it is fine with you.

It's like you are the blue sky. Birds come and go. Clouds come and go. The sky never really changes. It holds everything.

It's about being roomy. Roominess is the whole goal. You have so much room inside you, so much acceptance, that you can easily hold whatever furniture you have, the furniture of your life.

You are the wave and the ocean. You exist both in duality and in unity.

Isaac stopped and just looked at all of us. Silence and relaxation, open eyes. We all relaxed into spaciousness.

"That's it," he said. "It is this. The energy in this room is better right now than it was during the whole meditation."

13 Trust in God/ Baal Shem Tov

Rabbi Israel ben Eliezer was an 18th century mystic with a zest for God, for Life, for everything and everybody in the natural world. His perspectives revitalized the oppressed in Eastern Europe and gave birth to Hasidism. Deeply loving and beloved, he became known far and wide as the Baal Shem Tov, meaning "Master of the Good Name" (his acronym, the "Besht"). Miracles often unfolded through him.

One day the Baal Shem heard a divine voice telling him to go to a certain town to learn a lesson about trust in God. He and his students went there, found an inn, took their meal. As they were eating, a sheriff came in aggressively and slammed his club on the table three times. Then he walked out.

The innkeeper wasn't perturbed, but having a good time with his guests. He told them today he would get three such warnings that the rent was due.

The visitors said, "Don't feel obligated to wait on us, if you need to go."

"Oh, yes, I'll be going, but not just yet. I don't have the rent money yet."

After a little time, the sheriff appeared again, slammed his club on the table three times, and left.

The Baal Shem and his students marveled that the innkeeper was so relaxed. "Aren't you concerned?" they asked. In these times, if the rent wasn't paid, he and his whole family would be thrown into the Squire's dungeon.

"God will provide," he told the Baal Shem. They started to wonder if he was a little crazy.

After the sheriff came and slammed his club down the third time, the innkeeper dressed in his finest clothing. He started walking toward the Squire's castle with not a penny in his pocket. The Baal Shem and students went out on a balcony to watch him.

In the distance a carriage came along, stopped, and spoke with the innkeeper, who soon walked on. Then the carriage turned around to go back to him. They saw money exchanged. Both parties went on their way.

When the carriage reached the inn, the group asked the traveler what had happened. The traveler had just decided to buy the innkeeper's next batch of winter vodka, and paid him ahead of time. He said the price was steep. At first it seemed too much. But this was great vodka every year. And he knew the innkeeper was always an honest man. So he turned the carriage around and paid what he'd asked.

Later the innkeeper told them he had refused the first price because it simply wasn't enough for the whole rent, and he knew God would provide the whole rent bill.

Deep trust in God.

There are two ways of being in the world: one is the world of time where you accomplish things by planning, and you know what to expect because of what has happened in the past.

The second way is the world of only the Present, without a history, where anything is possible at any time. Here you know, without a doubt, the world arises from the will of God in each moment, and God does provide.

We tend to see everything through the filters of our history. Whatever way things usually go, we expect them to go that way again. In fact our thoughts color reality so much, that even as the Divine Will plays out in front of us, we don't even recognize it. It's happening right here, but our thoughts and our histories filter all the Divine Light out of it.

Take a look and observe this happening to you. I have watched myself doing it. My expectations are built on the past. I get distracted by my own history. My mind goes off-track from the Present moment of infinite possibilities. I sink.

When this happens we have to use our determination and "holy chutzpah." We sit down, quiet ourselves, reframe and refocus to the Divine Reality that everything in this moment is arising directly from God. No matter what is happening.

Don't make typical presumptions. Don't assume anything. Don't cover up this Present moment with the haze of old filters. Every detail arises from the mind of God. Literally anything is possible at any moment.

If and when we realize this, we also realize that we are nothing. Everything is God passing through us. We don't judge what happens.

Everything is "Gam zu l'tovah" - This too is for the good.

All of it, for the higher good, toward higher happiness for all. Everything is sunlight and more sunlight.

Let joy be your guide in this. Remember, the world is your mirror. So the more lightness and joy you bring to the mirror, the more lightness and joy will be reflected back to you. Your own kindness and trust in the universe will shine in your mirror, and you will likely be shown a kind and supportive world around you.

That's not to say you won't draw a wild card, once in awhile. Something crazy and difficult may pop up. But if it does, keep the faith. There's a reason for it, somehow. There's a bigger perspective. This too is for the good.

14 Pop into Divine Connection

After sweet expansive music and meditation, Isaac spoke about the writings of Ram Bam, Maimonides. In one work Ram Bam described the way God opens us to better connection with the divine. It's like God heats us up. Little by little. Hotter and hotter. To a point where we burst into a new level of understanding. A stronger deeper connection with God.

We might think of ourselves as kernels of popcorn that gradually grow warmer until we pop – into the divine insight. A kernel of popcorn looks inert. It looks like not much is happening. But the steady heat is beginning to change it, deep inside.

Many of us have felt this in our own life. Life events are working you over. Something inside you feels the heat building up. At some point, after more and more heat, you explode into insight. Your "A-ha" moment. This is your awareness, popping wide open to divine connection.

Question: How can I turn up the heat, so I will pop?

God is the one who turns up the heat. You don't. It's not your doing.

From our human perspective, we make efforts. We eventually gain clarity and connection. We observe what happened to us, and we think it's due to our own efforts. We think it's cause and effect, but it's really not. We put our framework on the experience. It's really God, gifting us with heat, popping, and connection.

Your effort doesn't really accomplish anything. Grace is always a gift.

We always have this dichotomy that says: God does everything, we don't. And yet, make an effort, be a better person. It's written all over the Torah. You'll notice the Torah changes its perspective constantly. It says "make an effort." It says "you're not in charge, you can't do anything."

However, you need to see that your impulse to learn, your desire to be here at meditation is the gift. God has placed in you the desire for divine connection. This desire is His gift to you.

Question: My mind was so busy during meditation, I never settled down. It was one thought after another. I feel like I wasted my gift.

Isaac replied that it was not a waste at all. Your being here is a gift; it's all you need. In fact, because you were able to witness your thoughts, witness your busy mind, this was a gift.

All growth happens through self-observation. All growth is given by God. It's beyond our control. You can pray, "God help me recognize my ego impulse versus my soul impulse. Help me recognize what's driving me."

By increasing the skill of observation, you will find deeper and deeper happiness. You can walk outside, look at the sky, and suddenly weep for joy because you see something in it you've never seen before.

The more present you can be, you'll find the present moment widens to include some of the past and some of the future. When the moment widens even more, you'll see more of the past and future. This is the beginning of the skill of prophecy. This is the way the sages attained such things.

Question: If my effort isn't effective to turn up the heat, and God helps me on His schedule, not mine, then why ask for help?

That's a good point, said Isaac. Some people come to a place where they simply stop asking for help. Also, asking for help can backfire on you. When you ask to be closer to God, it's like, "Sandpaper my ego, Lord." Ask that, and you're not going to like what you receive.

Yet you will eventually be drawn to jump into the fire of divine connection, no matter what it costs you. One day when life becomes too much of the same thing, or for some other reason, you'll have a strong impulse, and you'll leap. You want to be close to God. Your very desire to be close is God's gift to you as well.

We always have this dichotomy that says: God does everything, we don't – and yet, make an effort, be a better person. It's written all over the Torah. You'll notice the Torah changes its perspective constantly. It says "Make an effort." It says "You're not in charge, you can't do anything."

15 A Story of Karma/ A Story of Healing

Isaac told about a man who accidentally hit and killed a pedestrian. The pedestrian was an elderly man, maybe with Alzheimer's, who walked out in front of the car. It wasn't the driver's fault, but he felt intensely guilty. He could hardly live with himself. He did everything he could to make repairs, but still life was difficult.

Finally he wrote to a very wise and respected rabbi in Israel, telling about this situation and asking how to release himself.

The sage wrote back one word: "Amalek."

Amalek was the nation of people who chased the Israelites through the desert for 40 years. The nemesis of the Jews.

So the troubled man didn't know what to make of that. He already knew he was troubled, "chased," persecuted by his conscience. He filed away the letter and tried to get his life back to normal. He wanted to move to a new place and start over.

He found a new location in the same general area, a home he liked. When the papers were signed, the young couple selling it expressed their relief, because it had belonged to their father, who was killed some time before, hit by a car.

The man realized this was the very person he had hit. Oddly, he felt some resolution, as he lived in and cared for this place.

At some time later, he went down to the basement and found some old boxes filled with documents and photos. There was a photo of the elderly man when he was younger, wearing a Nazi uniform of high rank and standing next to Hitler. Not only that, but the documents included a list of all the people who'd been put to death under his orders. On the list were the names of this man's own father and mother. Justice was served.

So we don't know the big picture of karma, of divine justice. The sage could see the big picture, which is why he replied, "Amalek." The persecutor received his due.

Sages have managed to dissolve themselves so much that they have access to the big picture.

This is a lesson for us, because so often we yearn for justice. We think we need to go out and get justice ourselves. But we can't possibly know the bigger picture. We with our limited human vision cannot correct everything.

We need to give it to God. We need to let it go and trust in divine justice, which will always prevail.

Of course if it's a situation where we can actively repair it, apologize, forgive, make peace - we need to do that. But if it's beyond your powers, let it go.

Our focus is not to stay glued to old worry, resentment, or guilt. Our focus is to release, relax, and tune in to our divine connection. Nurture this.

Take care with relationships. Your relationship with yourself, with God, with others here on earth.

Here's a story from Swami Rama's life. At the age of about twelve, he traveled with his master, and they relied on others' kindness to supply their needs. Young Swami Rama was always hungry. One day at a train station, his master asked a clerk at the station if he might provide them with some food.

The clerk immediately closed up shop and led them to his home. Sages are so respected in India.

However the clerk's wife was upset. She said, "Our own son is dying of smallpox, and you want me to feed these two? Forget it. If they're so holy, maybe they can cure him."

So the master liked a challenge. He asked for a glass of water. He held the water and circled the boy's cot three times. He drank the water. The pox left the boy instantly, reappearing on the master's face.

Swami Rama was frightened. The master told him not to worry. They went out to a tree, where the master sat down. The pox went to the tree and disappeared from the master's face, then disappeared from the tree.

People were gathering, and the two sages hurried off to lose the crowd.

The master was big enough to take on the smallpox. When a sage evolves that far, it's easy to take on others' suffering and release it.

16 Ribnitzer Rebbe Releases a Lost Soul/ Deep Listening

Chaim Zanvl Abramowitz (1902-1995), known as the Ribnitzer Rebbe, was an extremely holy Hasidic tzaddik (saintly one). Born in Russia, he guided his people through Stalin's tight reign. He was devout, compassionate, and so fully surrendered to God that miracles surrounded him. In the last two decades of his life, he lived in the United States.

Isaac told a story of the Ribnitzer Rebbe, who was traveling in the desert between Arizona and California. A driver and some companions attended him. As the vehicle rolled through the empty desert, something important caught the Rebbe's eye.

He looked astonished. He told the driver, "Pull over – didn't you see him?"

They stopped, and the Rebbe went out to the roadside. It was the middle of nowhere. He stood out there and held a conversation with somebody invisible.

Then he came back and they went on their way.

The driver asked what that was about.

The Rebbe replied a lost soul had been wandering here a long time. He listened. He heard him out. He offered prayers and direction for him. He showed him how to go home, and he was happy to do it.

The Rebbe was so in tune, he had access to lost souls. He had more range in his vision than most of us do.

True deep listening is the highest holy skill.

See what happens when you fully give yourself in listening to a family member. How healing that is.

See how you feel, if you ever receive the gift of being fully heard by a good listener.

If we can dedicate ourselves to ten pure unblemished minutes of meditation each day, with deep listening to God, we will discover ever new depths in that quiet space.

Make your cup strong so it can hold whatever God may pour for you. You can't hold anything if the cup isn't secure, isn't whole. A strong cup will be able to receive the blessings.

All wisdom is a gift. We are just receptacles.

Our actions don't do much, but being Present does.

Isaac asked us to call up the deepest sense of comfort within ourselves. Forget our worries, put them off. He led us into a meditation that grew more and more sweet and expansive. He began to play songs on his guitar, and we joined in. It was the sweetest joy to sink into meditation, even while singing. The whole room expanded.

17 In the Beam of God's Loving Attention

As we've learned, said Isaac, there are two concurrent and contradictory ways of being in the world. One is attached to time and history, the way we define ourselves and our past, the cause-and-effect approach.

The other approach, as all spiritual traditions teach, is that this world is being created fresh in each moment. Everything that is happening is a product of Divine Will. God is constantly directing loving attention upon you, and thus you and your world unfold in each moment.

See yourself at the end of the beam of God's attention. There at the end of that beam, you are blossoming. See yourself there. Turn and look at your Creator. See the line of boundless love, broken only by your distraction or lack of attention.

This beam of alignment between you and God exists only in the present moment.

This is the meditation practice today, if you choose to follow it. See yourself blossoming in that ray of love. See the connection between you and God.

(Silent meditation . . .)

God is creating us anew each moment. Anything is possible. It is God's constant loving attention that makes us exist at all.

Question: Does God stop thinking about me when I cease to exist on this earth?

No, Isaac replied. The Nefesh, the physical body/soul doesn't actually die, but is drawn into the Ruach, the astral body/soul. Each level is drawn into the next higher level as we evolve. None of the levels of soul ceases to exist. Rather, they are drawn up, the way an extended telescope can collapse, while still containing all the concentric tubes within it. All parts are still there.

God continues to gaze upon you. Your joy arises when you return that gaze.

The Ancients tell us the One becomes many, for this interaction, this interplay of God looking upon Itself. God revealing Itself to Itself.

God becomes you talking to me, in order that both people can realize, in this connection, that both are God. This sweetness is the whole point of creation. It is in these moments that God reveals Himself.

There's a relationship between the seer and the seen. When they meet, they find each has attributes of the other. This connection, this alignment happens only in the present moment.

We're here on earth to experience the sweetness of this connection.

A mitzvah (good deed) done in joy ("tanug") makes alignment and connection through all worlds. It opens the pipelines from the worlds above to the worlds below. All the valves are opened, all the way down into our dense and lowest world here. Our joyful kindness brings joy to all worlds. Those "higher up" benefit from our actions. Imagine that.

But Heaven opens only for the mitzvah done in joy. A good deed done out of obligation doesn't carry so much divine energy.

The connection and alignment we're talking about has to be in the now moment. It's not the song or the singer. It is the singing. The working. The loving. Always in present tense.

18 Ribnitzer Rebbe/ Hearing Torah

For a time Reb Yakov served the Ribnitzer Rebbe, an extremely holy tzaddik (saintly one). In the middle of the night the Ribnitzer Rebbe told Yakov, his driver, that they had to go immediately to a different town, to help clarify some piece of scripture.

So off they went. It couldn't wait till morning.

The Rebbe read a holy book while Yakov drove.

He asked Yakov to drive faster. Faster! This is urgent.

At the same time the Rebbe was telling him about the book.

Yakov felt nervous, as his teacher kept talking and teaching, while at the same time demanding more speed, more speed. Yakov had the gas pedal floored, and it wasn't fast enough. Even worse, they were approaching the most dangerous part of the road, several miles of treacherous curves. Cars always went off the cliffs here.

Suddenly the Rebbe demanded, "Look in the book!"

Yakov tried to glance at it, but couldn't tear his eyes off the road, as fast as they were going, with the curve looming ahead.

"Look!" the Rebbe ordered him, shoving the pages closer.

In that situation, you are bound to your teacher, bound to obey. It's a challenge, a test. Could he pass this spiritual test, or whatever it was, even in this perilous moment?

"Look in the book!"

As desperate as Yakov felt, he decided to look at the page. Then came a long moment. His eyes stayed on the page longer than he'd intended.

When he turned back to look at the road, it was straight and calm. He knew they were suddenly many miles further. The curving treacherous cliffs lay behind them. They had zipped ahead, by miles, in an instant.

So you see, a tzaddik goes beyond natural law sometimes.

Shavuot celebrates the giving of the Torah.

We hold that the Torah is the mind and word of God.

When God offered the Torah to them, the Israelites agreed: "We will do and hear." The Hebrew word for hearing carries the connotation of "tanug" – joy.

They agreed to be the hand of God, doing His will, understanding that this itself would bring joy.

A mitzvah done in joy connects all worlds.

God is hiding in all worlds – hiding behind a screen.

The screen is your confusion.

Your joy connects worlds.

Your sadness breaks them apart.

The hearing of Torah, which is divine teaching in any form, will give us joy.

Joy for no reason at all.

Don't attach a reason to this joy. Not even a spiritual reason.

This joy just IS.

It's a joy that's in you for no reason, bubbling up spontaneously.

19 Pond of Ripples, Pond of Stillness

When we talk about meditation, we often use the metaphor of a pond or a pool of water. We want to make our mind quiet, like a still pond.

Every thought arising is like a stone cast into the water. It disturbs the water with a splash. Then it creates ripples, touching many other tangents, many other thoughts unfolding from the first one.

If our pond always has ripples, then we won't notice the subtlety of a pebble dropping into it. It takes a big boulder splashing in to get our attention. Only the big splash can be felt.

If our mind always carries turbulence, restlessness, then we may never notice, never hear or see anything that arises from the subtle realms beyond this one. We need a much deeper stillness inside, if we want to be aware of the subtle realms. And each realm is even more subtle than the last.

When we can find more stillness, the first thing that happens is, we gain insights during meditation. Some people like these insights so much, they stay there in the world of insights. But there is more to be perceived if we continue deeper into stillness.

Stay aware. Don't fall into sleep. Sleep is natural, but it's the temptation we must overcome. Sleep is an escape from what we don't understand.

We need patience to get to these deeper quieter realms. Patience will eventually overcome anything – and everything. Stay in your seat and keep listening to the quiet. Keep meditating for the allotted time. Build this muscle of meditation.

The soul has an innate contentment and comfort.

Contentment is the opposite of waiting. Waiting in traffic, waiting in line, waiting for a better day. If we're waiting it means we're not satisfied with where we are right now.

The more we can simplify our needs, the easier life becomes.

What's difficult is that inner restlessness so common to most of us.

So call up within yourself that sense of comfort.

Sometimes you may be amazed at the sweetness of one full breath.

When you release that breath, when you let it go, it feels even sweeter.

Call up that contentment within you now. Let it build. Let it spread throughout you.

20 "I am" Meditation Practice/ Inner Witness

A sage named Nisargadatta Maharaj gives a simple teaching, based on witness consciousness. No matter how young or old you are, no matter what turmoil or sweetness you go through, there is a Self that is always with you. This Self never changes. It watches with a loving eye. It loves all it sees. It is the part of you that joins together your many experiences. If you didn't have It, you'd think you were being reborn each day to a different life. This Self joins together all the events and stages of your life, so you can say things like, "when I was young" or "when I was dreaming." It is your basic awareness.

The way to bring this Self forward is to simply meditate on the feeling in your heart that "I am." I exist, I'm here. Don't meditate on the words or the thought, but on the feeling. I'm here.

Nisargadatta meditated many long hours on this. Through this alone he found enlightenment. This is all you need.

The mind leads to thought which creates emotion. Emotion sucks you into the world of story, and by then you are asleep, drugged into the ordinary world.

Hooks of desire and worry keep you immersed in this world.

Unhook yourself, step back, and see. The continuous truth is "I am."

21 Bliss Orbit Meditation Practice/ Just Be

Imagine yourself as consisting of several planets and orbits. The sun of enlightenment is in your center. The furthest away planet is the physical body, orbiting out there. Next planet inward is the emotional body. Further in from that is the mental-thinking body. More interior is the bliss-body. Bliss is still not enlightenment, but it lifts you to happiness when you're in it.

Finally at your deepest core is the sun, true enlightenment without personal identity.

You have all these bodies all the time, whether you visit them or not.

Even if you have never felt bliss, you do have a bliss body. It is available always.

Here's the suggested practice in the coming weeks. When you sit down to meditate, check in with each of these bodies.

Start with the outer orbit. How's my physical body? Feels okay. How are my emotions? Fairly stable. How's my mind? As busy as ever.

When we relax into deep quiet, we visit the bliss orbit.

Yet we are mostly mental people. It's like we have a rubber band attached to the mental world. We may visit bliss, but the rubber band keeps snapping us back into thinking.

We keep slipping into the orbit of thoughts.

Good thoughts give rise to good times. Bad thoughts give rise to bad times. Yet if we release thoughts and go more inward to live in the sheath of bliss, then we don't care about good and bad times. Good/bad doesn't make such a big impression on us, because we have the stability of bliss. We're not so impressed with our health or lack of health, our wealth or poverty. Our priorities change. We disengage. We don't take things personally. We prefer returning to bliss.

Practice now going into bliss. Now is the time, as we are coming into a world shift toward peace. When more people live in the bliss orbit, there is no more urging toward peace, because peace is the very air you breathe. It's not an issue.

Those sages who have lived in bliss always had a smile playing about their lips. It's a happy place to live. It makes everything in your view appear blissful, no matter the circumstance.

Yet we can easily see that in our world now, in the mental world, people are in constant conflict, striving toward peace. Struggling. You see it on the news. This is the thinking world. Not peaceful.

The mind was designed to create problems and to solve them. So the mind will always have problems. It needs problems. It wants to chew on them. That's what it does.

Also. The mind takes this teaching as information, as a key to use later. Don't save it for later. That's missing the whole point. Why wait to open the door, when you can open it now? All learning occurs now. It's not for later.

Learn now to let go, to release into a state of contentment. Breathe.

Those in the bliss world have learned to use intuition, which is a higher intelligence than the mind.

In the outer orbits of body, emotion, mind, a person may be flapping around crying out: "It's the end of the world!"

But in going to bliss orbit, a person can observe happily and simply say, "It's not my world." It is what it is, and I don't take it personally. It's not my role to fix it. Not right now. I accept that God has charge of all of it.

You won't lose touch with your practical life. All of that continues. You still need to do the practical things. But you won't take life so seriously.

Imagine yourself having worked a long time to go on vacation, and now finally you're in Hawaii, on your towel, on the beach. What do you do then? Do you think about it and keep planning how it could be better? Resting on the beach, do you struggle over what's for dinner? The best approach is to simply stop thinking and feel it, be it, soak in it. You are speechless. You touch your heart. You simply love it.

When you fully connect with your surroundings, you don't label and reframe and think it all out. You simply embrace it. You want to BE the tree, BE the beach. When you lie on the beach, soaking in all the sights and sounds and tastes, the only proper response is, "Ahhh."

This is the learning. Go to the place in you that simply says "Ahhh." No words. Just, "Ahhh." You have arrived.

This is a way of being. Not doing. Not thinking. Not information. Just, Ahhh.

22 Your Life Purpose/ Four Archangels, a Bedtime Practice

What is your life purpose? You can find it by looking at two things.

Look at a gift or talent you have been given that is specific to you.

Look at a recurring problem or difficulty that teaches you better control or growth.

Part of the growth for Moses was to learn to control himself. As a young man, he was afraid of no one. His anger lashed out at the mistreatment of the Israelites. He had no problem killing somebody to get rid of an obstacle. As he aged, he went through extreme inner growth to control his murderous desires. After growth and more growth, special grace was given him. He had done so much inner work that miracles happened for him, such as parting the waters of the sea.

We can't all be Moses. But we each have a unique role to play on this earth. We come here eager to play our role. So eager, we want to go straight to the front of the class, with no work, no preparation. We're eager for the end result. We get caught in this long view, often imaginary, instead of the short view which addresses practical growth for this day now.

Habitually we dwell on the future - what will I become in twenty years? We want to ignore the step that's right in front of us. We don't want to deal with our immediate task at hand.

We each have some task, right now today. The angel Uriel kindly lights up our next task for us, shows us what is needed now.

Have you ever climbed a mountain on a wet, slippery path? You had to focus only on the step you were taking that moment, not any future step. You had to make sure the footing underneath you was secure before putting your weight on it. Then you had to choose only the next step. Otherwise you would slide down. The path you wound up taking was not the one you had anticipated, because of all the slippage.

So too in life we have to think only about this current step. Is it secure? Is this what I should be doing right now? That's more than enough to be thinking about, in this moment.

(Isaac strummed his guitar and spoke about the Archangels before singing a song about them.)

Each night when we go to sleep, it's considered a little death, as we are going to the next plane. So we ask Michael to be on our right side, the side of Chesed, love, giving. Gabriel to be on our left side, the side of Gevurah, strength, discipline.

A word about Gevurah. So many people find it difficult to say no. They go along with everything, and others walk all over them. This isn't balance. You must learn to say no.

And how do you say no?

"No." Open and frank. Not with anger. Just, "No, not today." If they ask you again, say, "No, not today." As many times as it may take.

Don't wait to say no. Don't repress your honest reply. Don't save up your anger and explode all over them. Such anger can build big and then explode over a small thing. Don't drop an atom bomb to blow up an outhouse.

It's just "No."

If you can't say no to others, it means you don't know how to say no to yourself. The outer world mirrors the inner.

As we said, we invite Michael on our right, Gabriel on our left.

Uriel is before us, lighting our way, illuminating and guiding us, just one step at a time. Only one step, no more. All you really need to see is the next step.

Raphael is behind, the doctor. Why is the doctor behind you? He's whispering in your ear that the struggles in front of you really came from your past.

Shekhinah, the Presence of God, rests above your head.

As you drift to sleep, invite them in. Feel them supporting you into sleep.

23 Swami Rama/ Be the Witness/ There's Nothing Wrong

Swami Rama (1925-1996) was an Indian yogi, humanitarian, teacher, and writer. One of his many stories is about a time he went to learn from a sage. As soon as he met him, the sage announced Swami Rama had come too late. He wouldn't be able to teach him, because he was due to die the next day. Sure enough, the sage died as predicted.

Swami Rama stayed on a little longer. He observed as different religious groups came forth to claim the sage's body and honor it with their most sacred burial. The Christians arrived to take his body. Just then the Moslems showed up and claimed their right to him. The Hindus asserted that they had precedence. Representatives of all three sects stood over his body, their argument heating up until they were shouting at each other.

Suddenly the sage woke up and said, "Enough!"

It's a lesson to remind us no religion is greater than any other. Every sect puts together their unique formula, and claims it's the best way to find the Divine. They're eager to proselytize. They welcome you in and give you good news for your soul. Provided you follow their rules. But the entry into most religions is a one-way door. They want to invite you in, but they don't want to let you go out. It's a sticky situation. They need you more than you need them, in some cases.

At the beginning of the spiritual journey, many of us need doctrine, dogma, rules to help us on our path. But eventually the path becomes less rigid.

Anybody looking for Divine connection can find it. Unlimited by dogma. In fact all roads, no matter how winding, lead us Home. Each of us, someday, no matter how much we get sidetracked, no matter how many wrong turns we take in how many lives, will eventually find our way back to God.

Patience. We learn patience through the eons.

Little by little we may let go of the ego.

How much can you surrender?

Become God's instrument. When you learn to do this, people will grow to love you even more. Nobody really likes a dramatic person who is constantly thrown about by their own suffering and talking about their own woes.

Go to the position of the Witness. When you are the Witness, you gaze upon everything with equanimity. Nothing is more important than anything else. The Witness does not see any benefit. Because everything is already fine, just as it is.

The ego constantly says what is better and what is worse. The ego is driven by anything that benefits it – even a spiritual path. Watch out when the ego says, "Look at me on my great spiritual path. I'm getting good at this. Look, I'm losing my ego. I'm so evolved." That ego only went underground, and it might be stronger than ever. Don't let it hijack you.

Be the Witness, who simply experiences and embraces what is, just as it is. No benefit.

If the thought is tied to any benefit, it is ego-driven.

This being at peace with what-is, this Witness filled with Presence, is what heals us.

No resistance. Drop all resistance, and your body, mind, heart, naturally rebalance themselves. They return to good health.

Try a new approach. Wherever you go, remind yourself: "There's Nothing Wrong here."

24 We are a Bottle in the Divine Ocean/ Inner Witness

Each of us is like a bottle of ocean water, corked, and floating within this endless divine ocean. Surrounded and filled by this divine water, most of us are unaware of It.

God is within and without.

Each of our personal bottles is filled with the same ocean.

Each bottle has its own color, shape, texture. Each comes into form differently. So we perceive the differences from one person to the next. But each holds the same sea water.

The sea water gives life to the bottle.

The sea inside is the bottle's very life, poured into form.

The cork in the top of the bottle closes it off from the rest of the sea and makes that bottle feel independent and separate.

That cork is actually made of our thoughts. In fact it grows thicker, the more thinking we do.

Our busy thoughts separate us from the divine.

If we were able to change our cork into a screen, to minimize our thinking and just Be, then we would feel more of the sea flowing through us. A screen allows the sea to come and go, refreshing the bottle.

In the same way, the window at our crown allows God in.

Memory is really designed to reinforce the continuity of the small self.

If we could release memory, we would change our cork into a screen.

People tend to let their past rule their present. They've had trouble, and they assume more trouble is on the way. They can't let go of their recurring memory of trouble as a way of life. And we would have to say, okay, it's still sleeping time for them.

Even in meditation you can feel your memory pull at you. Your monkey-mind reaches back into your history to grab the fruit of fear or desire.

Try to gain distance on your small self's story. Imagine you are on a mountaintop, and far off down there somewhere is little Isaac with his little-self problems.

The ego tends to hijack the divine Witness in so many ways. It even hijacks our spirituality and takes credit for it. We say, "I'm so good, look how good I am."

But "good" is just one half of duality, where our ego is at work.

The Witness isn't cold. It's warm, loving, compassionate. The fully present Witness brings healing, because it brings God to that moment. The Witness knows everything is from God, all the time.

The Witness knows nothing is wrong. Nothing is ever wrong.

25 Blessings and Curses/ God infuses All/ God is One

Isaac read from the parsha (Torah Portion) of the week: "You shall have blessings and curses."

"And right away we have a problem," he said. "Because God is all good."

God is not sending curses. To see something as a curse - this is our own perception of it.

Light is only good. But light takes the form of the vessel it is poured into, just as water does. Perhaps it's a round cup or a square cup. One is revealed blessing and looks good. The other is concealed blessing and looks not good, looks like a curse to us.

Whether it looks like a blessing or a curse, it is still God infusing everything.

How often we forget that God infuses all. Or perhaps we haven't realized this yet. Perhaps we have stayed on the bottom floor of our metaphorical building, where our view is narrow, where we think we have the answers, where we think we are alone, struggling to build our life with our own effort.

Some athletes, when they win, they thump their chest and yell about their great victory. It's all about winning. "I did that." There's an arrogance. "I'm smart, I'm great, I'm all-powerful."

But watch out, because as soon as you think it's you doing these things all by yourself, the tide will turn, and your vessel will compress you. Life will become not so easy, as a way to teach you that you're not in charge.

God comes through us. It's not us doing these things.

Sometimes it takes awhile to learn that our blessings are Gifts to us. They are not our possessions.

The Sh'ma, which we may say on arising in the morning and several times throughout the day, tells us our core belief: God is everything and fills everything.

The English translation of the Sh'ma is, "Listen, Israel, (you who struggle with God, or you who go straight to God) - the Infinite (YHVH) is our God, the Infinite (YHVH) is One and Only One."

Can we hear this? Can we see it?

In Hebrew, the word for "see" is "re'eh." This word comes from Chochmah, or Wisdom. The word for "listen" is "sh'ma." This word emanates from Binah, or Understanding.

Chochmah and Binah are the highest attributes of the bodily sefirot, before we reach the top, Keter, the crown above the head, which is incomprehensible union with the Divine.

We need to see with Chochmah, see with Wisdom, that the "curse" is only our perception regarding the shape of the vessel we look upon. See that all vessels arise from God.

We need to listen with Binah, listen with Understanding, that the Infinite is One.

Echad means 'One' not as a number but as wholeness, completeness. God is the Whole. God is Complete. God is All. There is no other.

The letters of Echad add up to the number 13. The word Ahavah, love, is also 13. So the whole of everything is filled with love, filled with light, despite the vessel that we see here. Whether that light is concealed or revealed, it is still light.

God didn't create the world and then say, "That's not so good." It's all good.

We have the responsibility to make ourselves into light-revealing vessels.

We can try to hide. The thief thinks he isn't seen. "I can just get away with this," he says, "no one's looking." But there's no hiding. Everything is seen by God. You can steal for only so long. You will later pay in some way. You will become the victim and have things stolen from you.

There was a young man filled with confidence and strength. Everything he tried came easily to him. He was a tremendous financial success from the age of fifteen. He later created a company and made a million by the time he was twenty-two. But at that age, the money didn't last long. He was young and had so many desires. He bought everything he wanted and enjoyed it. But fortune turned and the money ran out. He tried a new venture, and it took off, but it failed. He tried again, looked like success, but soon failed.

His vessel was being twisted into concealment. He failed time after time so he could learn that blessings are Gifts. His great confidence in himself was tested.

There are two kinds of confidence. The typical confidence says, "I'm great, I can do anything." The higher confidence simply has faith that everything is for the good, and I am not in charge. Gam zu l'tovah. "This too is for the Good."

We tend to think our actions are bringing blessings to us. That is not so. Everything comes from God. Everything arises from inside us and is projected outward into the mirror of the world.

When we look into a mirror we know that's our own image. But imagine a primitive person might think it's someone else in there, and start to talk to their image as if it's somebody else. This is the way we usually project our inner stuff to the outside world. Whatever we see "out there" is really coming from inside us.

We think our problems are exterior, but they're interior. For example, we may feel loneliness. We search the world for a mate to cure our loneliness, but all we do is cover it up. We are still lonely inside. The problem didn't go away.

We carry our problem, don't we? We declare that this is a problem. We make it into a problem. We start telling our friends and creating our story around it. I don't like this problem. It's bad. Now we are putting that issue into concealment. We might call it a curse.

It's a concealed blessing.

> So right now, feel your contentment. Breathe.
> Feel how nothing is missing.
> Feel God inside you, filling you.
> This is what you are.
> This is all you are.
> God is One.
> God is All.
> You need nothing.
> It's all right here, within you.

When you realize you already have everything you need, then your old desires become meaningless to you. You might find yourself wanting to go back to the way things were, the people you used to hang out with, the places you used to go. And maybe you go back and try it, but it just doesn't mean what it used to mean.

Any time you feel a challenge coming on, if you can reach first for that contentment inside of you, for that deep awareness of God in you, then you won't have to go down the old path and be pulled by your fears and desires.

There's also the step-down teaching. If you can't find contentment inside, you can try another method. This is the method of bestowal. For instance, if you feel poor, give charity to someone poorer than yourself. You say, "So now I have even less." But in bestowing, you are touching that vibration of divine giving, which will open more abundance for you. You may feel you have absolutely nothing left to give, and yet if you can do it anyway, it will make a difference for you.

Using this method of bestowal, you should try to give whatever it is you are lacking. This will help open the door for your own healing.

Question: Is it better to use prayer to ask for things or to just give thanks?

Beginners' prayers, like the ones we teach children, are all about asking, and this is fine. We ask God to soothe our fears and give us our desires. We don't feel complete. We ask for things so we can feel complete.

But somewhere down the road of spirituality, you will find yourself in meditation where there are no words at all. Here you simply connect and feel complete with God. No words are needed.

26 Ayin-Nothing and Yesh-Something

Isaac guided us into meditation. Silence.

He then urged us to see ourselves in the state of contentment (Ayin, nothing).

Then compare it to the energetic shift of thinking (Yesh, something). Feel inside, feel the difference between these two states. Shift and feel "contentment." Shift and feel "thinking."

The Neshama always feels content. This contentment is the larger part of you. It is formless. It can't be contained in your body. You are always in touch with it.

All sensation is created by Elokim - God in the world of form, infusing a multiplicity of forms. In this dualistic ego world, Elokim is at work with a constant flow of sensation and contrast, pain and pleasure.

Havayah is the name of God's Essence in the realm of the Neshama, the soul, where spaciousness and nothingness (Ayin) abounds.

Havayah is the sun, and Elokim is the shield.

God is concealed behind the shield of sensation in this world of form.

Go now into contentment. Breathe.

Let go the way a fist uncurls.

Release and know that you will not lose whatever you are grasping.

It won't drop far. Just release.

The Garden was a place of contentment, a place without good or evil. To the Neshama there is no evil, and no good either. Everything just is.

But then we saw the attractive fruit of Elokim, of sensation and comparison, of good and evil. We chose to try the fruit. We saw good and evil. We became more and more taken by it. We went into the story of it. We began to see the earthly world as more real than the Garden. The more we were interested in the earthly fruits, the less contact we felt with the Garden. But the Garden is always here. Havayah is always available.

It's as if the Neshama (Soul) stepped in too close and merged with the small self. Similar to the way we might cry at a sad movie, or get scared at a horror film, or fall in love with a love story.

See your sensations arise. That's Elokim. Yesh. Something.

Now go back to contentment - Havayah. Ayin. Nothing.

Feel the difference.

This is the union of Ayin and Yesh. When the two unite, they make a bridge where blessing flows. Blessing is formless. It flows through this bridge into form, becoming whatever that blessing is meant to be for you. Whatever is needed will be formed from the formlessness.

Elokim runs every detail here on earth. We may think we are doing things. We aren't.

You are blossoming in the beam of God's attention.

Let go and realize your actions are not running your life. Don't fear losing your character. Your character will go on. It will do what it will do, without the force of ambition.

At death we lose all sensations. Sight, sound, smell, taste, touch – each dissolves away. And we return to our formless Neshama.

Why not learn to go there now? Learn to relax those sensations. We are not the body.

If we're too attached to the body, when it comes time to leave this plane, we might not be able to fully release our form.

So relax here a moment.

Imagine this release. Return yourself to formlessness.

27 Maggid of Mezritch/ The First-day Light of God

Isaac told the story of an earnest man on his way to see the Maggid of Mezritch, but the sun was setting, and he had to choose to either stop and pray outside of town where robbers lurked, or to keep going into town without praying. He listened to his conscience and stopped, walking a short way to do his prayer in privacy. Meanwhile his faith in coming to no harm conflicted with his belief that robbers might get him.

After his prayer, he returned to the road to discover his wagon and horse had been stolen. But at least he had his life. He was okay. He hurried into town on foot and went straight to the Maggid.

There he complained that his wagon was taken, and how unfair that was, as he did the right thing and offered his prayers. The Maggid didn't usually use his second sight in such worldly matters, but he wanted to give the man some comfort, and in fact he could see exactly where the wagon was. So he told the man where to go, what the landmarks were, to find his wagon. He even said it hadn't been emptied yet. All his possessions were still in it.

The man went to the place described, and there stood his wagon. The robber was amazed and didn't even put up a fuss. "How did you find me?" he asked.

The man told him, and the robber wanted to go see the Maggid. So the two of them returned to the Maggid.

The robber expressed his amazement to the Maggid, but then asked, "You've been given this gift of sight, but isn't it to be used only on holy pursuits?"

The Maggid replied that he did use it almost exclusively on the study of Torah, but occasionally he looked around the world to find lost things.

At the beginning of the Torah, on the first day God said, "Let there be light." On the fourth day He created the sun and all the lights in the sky. Sages realized that these are two different kinds of light. The first-day light is the light of God, the energy that fills everything in the world. Whereas the light of the sun is earthly. Sunlight casts a shadow, and shows the light and dark, the duality of our world.

But the first-day light is holographic. It fills everything. And every bit of the world is inside every other bit. This is the meaning of holographic: each piece contains the whole of everything. This is how the Maggid was able to find the lost wagon. He just tuned in deeply to examine the hologram.

This energy, this first-day light is nonlocal and holographic. Everything is actually inside of you. Let's say a holographic plate reveals a 3-dimensional picture of an apple. When that plate is broken, every fragment of it also reveals the same apple.

Time and space always arise together. That's duality.

The larger part of you doesn't exist in the time-space dimension. The larger part of you is formless. You are formless. You aren't the person you think you are in this body.

When Isaac was in the Yeshiva, he liked to do his morning prayers with a quiet community of elders. In particular he observed the deep devotion of one man who was so very soft and gentle in his ways. Just watching him was an education. The man was filled with the light of the first day.

How often we forget about that holographic divine light.

Our mind runs toward complaints.

Solomon himself spent a long time being depressed about this world. He even wrote a whole book about it, Ecclesiastes. He said nothing is new under the sun. He goes on and on in bleak tones about how discouraged he feels. And he was a very wise man.

Under the light of the sun, eventually everything is taken away from you. You may start out young and strong, but as time goes by, you grow weaker. You have a new pain here and stiffness there. You can fight it. You can exercise and buy a new face cream. But no matter what, you will lose this fight, and you know it.

We each have our own movie of life. When we identify with our character, we are deeper into the movie. Earth life. We live by the light of the sun, which casts shadows. Light and Dark. Duality.

But if we can find the first-day Light, we may be able to live in it, and wean ourselves away from the light of the sun.

We need to fill up with divine light in order to release the light of the sun and the world of desires and fears.

We need to first fill up with contentment, before we can give up our old attachments, our desires and fears. As Lahiri

Baba teaches, there is no give-away without a taking up. You can't give up your old habit until you take up a new habit. That new habit is contentment.

Shabbos (the Sabbath) is about this withdrawal from the world of duality. On Shabbos we are content, we are complete. We have no desires, no fears. I don't go anywhere on Shabbos. Instead the world comes to me, holographically. The world is inside me. I am a fragment of God. First-day light fills everything.

You can find this comfort no matter your circumstance. Take a breath and feel contentment in yourself. Nothing to do, nowhere to go. Contentment with this breath. And the next one.

28 Be the Divine Ocean

Any child can tell you God is in everything, but what does that mean?

Feel yourself as the ocean. Imagine yourself as a limitless ocean. Waves arise in the ocean but the waves are still the ocean. Waves are vibration. Waves are sensation.

There is no solid world. What we see is created inside our eye. Inside our mind. What we hear and feel arises inside and is projected outside.

Go back into the place of comfort, seeing yourself as this ocean.

When waves arise, know that this is simply sensation.

Try the practice of labeling each sensation as hearing or feeling or seeing. (These first three senses are plenty for beginners, although you could also do taste and smell.) Some sensations will be a blend. For instance, anger may be labeled "feeling" but also "hearing" because you tell yourself the story of why you are angry.

When you do the labeling of feeling, hearing, seeing, don't jump into the story. Simply label it and let it go.

These are the sensations we will release when we die. It's good to practice observing and releasing them now. You can say, "Oh that's something I'm seeing," without doing anything more about it.

The sages in India speak about "Sat Chit Ananda." Absolute Bliss Consciousness. "Sat" is Absolute Being, which never changes. "Chit" is consciousness. "Ananda" means bliss, which is the true eternal state of the Universe.

Chit is not only consciousness. Chit is the mind-stuff, the mental vibrations, of the Divine Mind. Chit is any form of vibration, whether it reaches us through our ears, our eyes, our skin. Hearing, seeing, feeling. These are sensations arising from vibrations.

We could define vibration as all sensation, all duality, all motion, all desire or fear. Vibration is the vehicle to carry things into form. From formlessness into form.

All worlds come into form through vibration. Even those worlds far 'above' us still carry vibration, duality, desire.

So imagine yourself as the whole mass of this great ocean, and somehow you decide to vibrate. Let vibration arise.

That vibration is Om.

Vibration always rises and falls above and below a midline. Maybe you've seen an oscilloscope, where the frequency is mapped out in a wavy line. We have our ups and downs, but the center line of evenness is always there, throughout. In the same way, the ocean is level and smooth despite its many waves.

Question: Why would God want to vibrate?

"Why" arises from the receptive dip of the wave. "Why" is wanting more, saying something's wrong.

When the line dips down below the midline, it creates a cup, a receptivity that wants to be filled. So you are receptive to trying to fathom the unfathomable. I don't have an answer to your question.

Question: What about our Ascended Masters, and those who help us on other planes?

They are no more connected to God than you are. Say you have a dream and this wonderful Being appears, hits you on the head with a stick, and you see beautiful lights. And you say, "Wow, I just had an amazing spiritual experience." Then you put this Master high above you, and even that stick becomes important, and you think you need all this. But you don't. You have the whole ocean of existence in you all the time.

We tend to transfer all wisdom and bliss onto that master, when we actually have access to it ourselves. It's available all the time. It never leaves.

It's not my bliss. It's just as much your bliss. You don't need me to get it for you.

Sometimes we are like the fish who can't find the water surrounding and filling them.

It's all One, this ocean. It's God, alone.

Tap into this perception. Be alone, be the whole ocean.

As scripture says, "God is One – there is no second."

29 Elul / Returning

In the month of Elul now, I approach my Beloved and my Beloved approaches me, nearer than at other times of the year. We are Returning. Turning our attention to the Divine.

We need to make an effort, make repairs, make apologies, make peace.

Imagine standing in front of mirror with your arms crossed. You're waiting for the person in the mirror to make the first move. So you stand there. You wait.

You have the illusion that you are separate from this person in the mirror.

Nothing's going to happen until you begin. Don't just stand there and wait for the Divine Beloved to make the first move. A mature lover knows they have to make the first move, or everything dies off.

When we have difficult times in this world, we know the divine pipes are clogged above us. We need to go way up high to open them.

So we raise our vibration. We lighten up.

When you feel attacked or feel troubled, do not engage in the conflict. Instead turn to silence and rise higher to the world of unity where nothing is wrong or right. No judgments on anything here, in this upper world.

Thoughts float around, ready to take form in creation. But these thoughts carry no charge, no opinion. This place is only the birthplace of thought.

Some people might say you're avoiding the issue, like an ostrich puts its head in the sand. No. This is different.

You are going to a world far above this one, where nothing is wrong or right. You put yourself out of the race, out of the conflict. You move out of Duality into Unity, union with All.

30 Ladder of Worlds/ Divine Pipeline/ Ego Separates Us

There is a ladder of many worlds, existing above us, so to speak. The other worlds learn and benefit from us just as we do from them.

When we access the timeless, which we are able to do when we go into Presence, that energy flows from our lowest world straight up to our Creator, beyond the highest worlds. Then the energy flows back down through all the worlds. This is what our Sages teach. This is what happens when we go into the mode of full Presence.

Most of the time, everything arises first in the world of Spirit and makes its way into the physical plane. So - even though all time is Now - we could say that events occur in the "worlds above" prior to the event happening here.

But in this instance, when we are fully Present and allowing divine connection, it happens here "first." Then it goes straight up to God, and that energy flows back down through all the worlds.

In this way our actions feed all worlds. So the inhabitants of all worlds are happy to help us.

The physical world is the furthest limit of God's creation. Think of God digging a well through more and more layers until He finally hits water, and that's us. Even though we are the densest layer, we are the culmination of Creation. Creation was made for us.

We are the outer limits, and we have the biggest potential separation from God. But at the same time, everything that happens in the well affects us, affects all worlds.

God is always present, omnipresent. Yet sometimes we feel separated from God. The ego is the biggest way God hides from us. The ego is the biggest screen that separates us from the divine.

You may find you are Present and connected, but after awhile you take a nibble on the cheese. "What do people think of me? How can I turn this situation to my advantage? How will I make money out of this?" Then your screen is up, and God is hidden from you. The ego took over.

You'll notice the ego is an artificial being. It feeds only on the past and the future. It cannot feed on the Present. It doesn't even exist in the Present, in the place of no-thought.

Question: Do the higher worlds still have ego?

Yes they do. All beings who have any sense of their own identity have an ego. Ego continues in all the worlds until the place of formlessness and no identity.

Even angels have a sense of ego, although theirs is fully surrendered to serve God. Angels have names. Angels have the identity of a butler. They are created to do God's will, and they run to serve. "Let me serve. I was created for this purpose and this only." Angels have no intentions but to do God's will.

Question: What about free will, progress, evolution?

Truly, from the penthouse view of our metaphorical building, there is no evolution at all. Everything happens Now. Everything is perfect as it is. No effort is needed.

All of our greatest mystics, when they reach their truest and highest visions, return to tell us that life is a dream, and everything we see IS perfection. God is perfection. Cannot be improved. Already perfect.

The sages don't want to dissuade us from improving ourselves, and yet the penthouse view says no growth or effort is needed. Our efforts are part of the dream. In reality all is perfect as it is.

31 Stand Together/ Multi-level Skyscraper of Consciousness

This is the last Shabbos (Sabbath) of the month of Elul, the end of our year. All the Shabbos of this whole year are contained in this Shabbos, the culmination of them all. You could also say this Shabbos is like a concentrate of the past year. Everything is in it.

We have the capacity to wonder. Years ago Sai Baba would stretch out his hand, and a stream of vibhuti, sacred ash, formed about an inch below his palm. Sai Baba simply manifested it from his open hand. Observing such a thing, we are filled with wonder.

Would a dog see this and wonder? A dog would only wonder if he could eat it or not.

As humans, we have the ability to wonder about things, to discuss and debate and reason. The next level we reach after wonder is faith. Not the blind-obedience many of us were taught, but actually real faith, which is the ability to see that we are all interconnected. That everything and everybody including yourself is connected to all.

Some might experience this as a connection to the land of Israel. At the Wailing Wall, even non-religious people might spontaneously weep because it touches something deep within.

When you know about your interconnectedness to everything, you belong to all of it. After that you can't dump your anger in an out-of-the-way place, because everything is you. Just like when you hammer a nail you take care not to hit your thumb. It's your thumb.

With a real sense of interconnectedness the outer world becomes like a dream. There is no division to separate you from anything.

A family is like a microcosm of that interconnection. Even a difficult family.

In today's parsha, it says everyone in the community is called to stand together, from the leaders to the children. Many levels of society are named in these lines, but at the end it says, "from the woodcutters to the water-drawers."

What an odd phrase. Why would they pick those particular occupations? Because it ought to be an all-encompassing phrase, like from old to young, rich to poor, wouldn't you think?

A rabbinical sage said "woodcutters" means yirah, fear. "Water-drawers" means ahavah, love. So the passage would read, "from fear to love."

This is a path all of us will take, from fear to love.

The woodcutter represents the way the mind separates and classifies, cutting things into pieces to sort them out. If we have to move a mountain we can only do it by thinking about one shovelful at a time. Otherwise the task overwhelms us. We cut food into bite-sized pieces for a little child. A good teacher cuts information up and feeds it slowly to the student. We can't handle all the information at once. We need to take our bites and reconstruct the whole thing in our own heads.

The mind also creates fear. You may remember the poem about the centipede whose hundred legs worked fine until he began thinking how to make them work. Sometimes we have too much focus, too much thinking. We need to relax and just be.

How many of us have had the experience of waking up exactly when we wanted to, without the help of an alarm clock? This shows that our inner witness can wake us. Yogananda said everybody on the path will need to learn to manifest in such ways.
(Paramahansa Yogananda, the Indian yogi who arrived in the United States in 1920, brought meditation and Kriya Yoga to the West and wrote <u>Autobiography of a Yogi</u>.)

Many years ago when Isaac's children were babies, he would wake up in the middle of the night about two minutes before the baby began to cry. One night he awoke, but no cry followed. He wasn't feeling well. He drank a glass of water, went back to bed. He practiced "Gam zu l'tovah," telling himself even though he was feeling bad, "This too is for the good." As he lay there trying to relax, his heart started feeling warmer. Next he felt a physical sensation, like an opening, of his heart. He began to feel better and better, soon bordering on a feeling of ecstasy.

Then he found himself pulled up through many worlds, many dimensions. In the uppermost one he sat at a table with a group of friends. It was his job to pop up into the next world, then come back and tell these friends about it.

The whole feeling was of going and returning, going and returning. He did this as easily as a bird takes off from a branch. He felt the next world as a place of immense power and aliveness. It was fully vibrantly alive. He was just a pinpoint of consciousness within it.

His table of friends was a place of no judgment, no good or bad. They wanted to know about the next place, and he was able to tell them.

We all contain the multi-level building of consciousness, many numerous levels. Maybe our elevator is rusty, and we can't reach some of the levels yet. We need to oil it up. Maybe we live on the third floor, and we can see all the way to the ground. We think we're pretty high up already, maybe we're at the top of everything? But no. There are levels we haven't seen yet.

Our mobility between levels, our elevator, is important. Turning our attention is the key to our mobility. Turning our attention changes our vibration. Our vibration allows us to move up or down on this elevator. But we cannot shift upward until we train our attention.

If we carry a lot of baggage, those painful stories about ourselves and our life, the elevator will sink, not rise.

You want freedom? Drop the baggage.

"Oh, but I like my baggage, this is my stuff."

You are deluded. Our old baggage makes a cloud around the present moment, a cloud which is difficult to see through.

Here at the end of Elul, we need to look at our fearful stories. Drop the old year's stories. Don't live in the same bubble you've lived in all year. Break out. Let all your bubbles pop.

Be Present to what's really here. Don't fall into the old story.

32 Sukkot - Lose Yourself in Joy

We think we are running the show, and we're not. It's like Mama's driving the car, and the baby is in the back seat with his fake steering wheel. When he turns left and the car happens to turn left, he thinks he did it under his own power. Not true. God runs everything down to the tiniest detail.

Living in a shack, a sukkah, for seven days teaches us how little we need in order to be happy. In fact many of us have gone through our closets and discarded our excess by now. We learn that "living light" without baggage is a blessing.

In the wilderness God provides everything. All we need do is follow the pillar of cloud in the day, the pillar of fire at night. Collect the manna in the morning. Only enough for that day. We are ever ready to do God's will, in the moment.

So the sukkah teaches us to be ready, to be on the move, listening for God's call.

The Torah says "Sh'ma Israel" – which means Listen. But what does that mean to us?

Be Present.

Let's say I have a million dollars and I just put it into an account for you, and I'm about to give you your access PIN, but I'm going to say it only once.

You're sitting there flipping your PEZ dispenser and wondering what's for lunch. But now your ears perk up. You're listening. You get fully focused to hear your PIN. In fact you're so tuned in I could say it super fast and you would catch it. That's the kind of listening we're talking about.

When we listen like this, God can come through.

A renowned rabbi always went to speak to his community in a state of not knowing what he was going to say. This is contrary to what you learned in college, to be totally prepared, fully researched, your outline nailed down, your words fine-tuned.

It's better to arrive without pre-planned words, because when we come together we are a whole organism with many needs. All of your needs and my needs.

By simply being present, the appropriate message comes through to answer all of us. We are given what is needed for all.

Sukkot is about losing yourself in joy. We are afraid to lose ourselves and yet we yearn for it.

The sages say that on Yom Kippur we lose ourselves through fear. On Sukkot we lose ourselves through love - Ahavah.

So you're having a dream. In this dream you're driving on a dangerous cliff-side road, following the curves. Suddenly despite your efforts the car goes sailing off the cliff. There you are in midair. How far do you go? Not all the way to the bottom. It's rare that you see yourself crash. And why is that? Your fear wakes you.

Have you ever had a dream of love or of something so wonderful that the delight of it wakes you? Those dreams turn out disappointing, in fact, because you wake up and lose that delight.

In both of these cases, you wake because the mind cannot maintain the normalcy of the situation. Your emotion is too strong to stay asleep. Strong emotion has that kind of energy, waking you up.

On Sukkot the heavens pour joyful emotion upon us. We drink it in and become energized with it.

You know what real joy, real laughter does for you. Laughter carries us away. When you start belly laughing, you lose yourself. How old do you feel when you're in a good laugh? No age. You're like three years old again. And it doesn't matter why you're laughing. You can't stifle it. The more you try to stop it, the worse it gets, till your sides ache and the tears are pouring out your eyes, and you don't care, it feels so good.

When you're laughing like that, you're not checking your watch. In fact you wouldn't care if you lost your watch.

Dancing is holy at Sukkot. Move those feet, even if you don't get out of your chair. For some people the music sinks in only as far as the brain. The brain says, "That's nice, let's talk about it." For others it reaches in as far as the heart. And for some it goes all the way down to the feet - they can't help but dance.

(More music, singing, dancing!)

33 Ribnitzer Rebbe/ Adam's World/ Go Vertical on Shabbos

The Ribnitzer Rebbe was a miracle worker. Everybody brought him problems, lots of problems. After people saw him, things got better for them, so they told all their friends. Soon the Rebbe was seeing lines and lines of people every day. But he took it on cheerfully.

The older he got, the slower he spoke. His students assumed he was getting senile. He overheard them, and he said to one of his closest friends: "What they don't understand is that I am being taken to higher and higher levels."

It takes time to consider all the perspectives of those levels. It's not senility.

The Ribnitzer Rebbe was so attuned, such a conduit for the divine. One Sukkot the weather was extremely damp, misting for days at a time. The students put a clear plastic tarp over the sukkah at night to reduce the moisture dripping inside. They removed it each morning when the sukkah was in use, because the Torah says the roof should be made only of leaves or palm fronds. This roof needs to breathe, let the air in.

One morning when the Ribnitzer Rebbe came into the sukkah to say the blessing, he opened his mouth and nothing came out. His students held him on either side and urged him on. Again he gave it all his effort, yet he could not speak. Again they thought he was flaking out because of his age. Then one of the students remembered the plastic covering was still on. No one had noticed, because it was clear. He hurried out and removed it.

Immediately the Rebbe was able to say a beautiful blessing. This was the degree to which he was attuned to God. When the situation wasn't right, he couldn't speak no matter how hard he tried.

The parsha this week is the beginning of the Torah, the creation of Adam. The first Adam was both male and female. Adam's heels were brighter than the sun. That is to say, even the lowest part of him was filled with light. Special light, higher and brighter than the sun. Adam stood so tall, from heaven to earth, and stretched from one end of the universe to the other. This means he contained the whole universe within himself.

He lived in perfection. He wanted for nothing. His reason for living was simply to exist for God. He had no other purpose.

Then along came the snake, and the tree of good and evil. We might think of that tree as being filled not with apples but with videos. Movies. Illusions. It is the tree of stories and illusions.

In Adam's world, one didn't consider good and evil, because it didn't apply. His was not the dualistic world. It was a world of union, unity.

But in that world of unity, one does consider the real and the unreal. If it's real you can rely on it. If it's an illusion, you don't bother with it.

So there was Adam, looking at this tree of illusions.

The snake enticed Adam by suggesting he would honor God even more if he went into this world of illusion and then dispelled illusion. He suggested Adam would fight his way out for the glory of God. The snake snagged a bite of Adam's ego here. All created beings have some ego, in all worlds.

Adam took the bait and bit into the illusion.

The trouble is, once you're in this world, you're in, and you can't see your way out of illusion.

In Adam's first world of perfection, there was no cause and effect. If something, say a bottle cap, were thrown into the air it might stay there or it might suddenly rain a hundred caps. Whatever was divinely determined would just happen.

But once we hook into the chain of cause and effect, then time and space arise. Then we think we know what will happen next. Then we are thoroughly inside the illusion.

Without cause and effect, everything is only what it is. In such a place there is no need to do anything. The only thing is to simply know that God keeps coming through. Honor all of it as it is. All of it is God, in the world of Union.

Life is not easy for us in the world of illusion. This is the horizontal world, where we buy and sell, join and disperse, struggle as we do, horizontally across the face of the earth.

We forget to go vertical and connect with God.

This is why, in our tradition, once a week, we stop our horizontal life and "do nothing." Shabbos (the Sabbath) is our day to reconnect with the Garden, with God. We do our best to stay in the vertical plane.

On Shabbos there are no courts, no judgment, no looking at others to see their wrongdoing. All the rules and regulations for Shabbos are not intended to warn you of punishment but to enhance your vertical connection. It's like you lift your arms to heaven to stay vertical.

Meanwhile the horizontal world, if you give it attention, can hit you like a truck and flatten you right out of the vertical. When horizontal world and business thoughts creep in, you just say no.

The sages say our vertical connection has to be refreshed on Shabbos. The least prescription for anyone is to take one day in seven for this refreshment. And the ancient continuous energy of Shabbos celebrated worldwide for centuries helps you stay vertical for that day. On Shabbos, you go to a state of acceptance. Everything is what it is. No judgment, no resistance.

At the end of Shabbos we sniff spices. And why do we do that? To strengthen our soul for the onslaught of the week to come. It's like the way you might prepare yourself for the end of a retreat, your re-entry into the world, which can feel almost painful sometimes. The sweetness of the spices reminds us that Shabbos will come again.

34 Handling a Trigger/ Paying what's Due

When we are faced with a trigger, we can flare up into our usual story about it, or we can make a higher choice.

It's so easy for us to go into our old story, simply because of habit. This is the way we always react, so we do it again. And part of it is our rationalizing, telling ourselves we are right, this is only fair, this person needs to hear this from me.

Or – taking an extra-deep breath – we can go into Chesed, into love. We can realize there is nothing wrong here.

Our belief in our own lack is what shuts us down and pulls us away from God. There are so many ways we feel we are not enough. We fail at this or that, or we lack the character, the skills, the aspects we really wish we had. We think we have all these holes in ourselves.

When somebody falls in love, their empty holes begin to fill in. Their places of lack are filled. That's why they feel so good, so complete, so euphoric. Love heals all their lack.

The ocean of divine flow, when we get a drop of it, we call it love. It's indescribable, really, but we know it as love. It puts us in a place where we are complete. We are lacking nothing.

When we are lost in our story, a friend might support us by listening and agreeing that we have it tough, commiserating with us. But a better friend says, "Quit telling your story." Because that friend knows you are so much more than your story. That friend sees you in your completeness, and you are beautiful, and you don't even need that story.

The prayer "Elohai neshama sh'natata bi tehorah hi" – says, "The soul You placed in me is pure." The soul is always with God. It exists in completeness with God. This is a foundational understanding. It is so important to get this:

We are whole and complete just as we are.

We do not lack anything at any time, no matter what seems to be going on here.

Question: How can we handle din, the difficult times when payment comes due for past actions?

People handle din in several ways. One is to refuse to recognize it for what it is. Refuse to pay it, and even blame others for the difficulty you are in, never realizing that you put yourself in that position and it's up to you to work your way out of it.

The second way is to recognize your own hand was at work in creating this difficulty, and you accept that you will pay. But you ask for credit. You agree to make smaller payments over time.

Then some people not only accept that their time to pay has arrived, but they are willing to pay the whole debt right now. Sometimes, because of their sheer willingness, God drops their debt, and they don't have to pay it after all. Of course there is no guarantee ahead of time, but it sometimes happens this way.

Yet another development can happen when we accept ourselves and understand our total worthiness. Then we unite with God, and in a sense we don't even exist anymore. Here the debt is dropped because the debtor no longer exists.

We keep repeating these teachings and keep listening to them. Repetition is important. You may say, "I've already heard that," or "I know that, you said it last week." But the key to it all is, does our behavior change?

35 World of Vibration/ Go Inward to Your Core

We define our body through our senses. I can feel, see, hear, taste, smell my body; therefore it is me. It seems to be who I am. But if we can develop our inner Witness consciousness, we realize the body is not us at all. We are a consciousness much larger than the body.

One morning we might have a great meditation. The sensation in our body feels wonderful. We tell everyone, "I" had a fantastic meditation. But we fail to understand that the place we visited is not "my" sensation. Rather, what really happened was that we touched the field of all sensation. We visited the pool of joy that exists for all.

When we experience real love or joy, it comes from the soul.

We know this whole world is vibration. Nothing solid is here. You might say, "Wait, I have my house, I have my car." But we know those are made mostly of space between molecules. There is really nothing here at all. We create everything with our minds.

The mind creates the world. It doesn't exist on its own.

There was an experiment with iron filings on top of a drum. The man made different sounds, and with each specific sound, the iron filings would form into a new image or pattern. These images were reproducible according to the sound. This is one way to see how all the world is vibration.

You are so much more than this body. This body is a remote vehicle for you. It's as if you sent a robot to this planet, and you're watching by remote viewing. Your larger soul is looking through the eyes of your robot on earth and having a taste of earth life. The soul wants to experience the physical world. But you get lost in the idea that this remote vehicle is you. It is not.

Wherever we focus our attention, energy grows. When we take on a personality with certain stories, a certain history, then a lot of constant energy builds all that up to the point where it's all so real and so important to us. But it's not. It's not real at all.

Our body sensations from all our nerves usually take an outward flowing path, bringing our attention outside to this chair, this scene, this hamburger.

But we can change that flow and bring it inward to our spine. We reverse the flow. We do this with our attention. Energy follows attention. At first it may seem like you're using imagination to do this, but soon you will feel the reality of it. Our thousands of nerves go into the spinal cord. So we pull in that energy. We focus on feeling our core, in the spinal cord.

Moses' staff was shaped like the letter "Vav" which also represents the central column of energy in the body – the spine. This is a hint to us. We should withdraw from the senses and go into the energy of our spine.

As we withdraw from the outer senses, those senses fall away. We become the inner Witness, which is eternal. This is an important skill, to become the Witness. To withdraw from the outer senses. This can prepare us to let go of the body when we die.

In these meditations, the brain waves get slower. We go into deeper states of consciousness. We go from alpha to beta to theta waves and more. Some yogis can be in all these states at the same time. Many rabbis have done the same.

Another way to talk about this shift of consciousness is to speak about dreaming. When we dream, we know the world is not real. We are always the witness in the dream.

During deepest sleep, we are revisiting our larger soul. We need that deep sleep. Without it we get sick or go crazy.

Question: Isaac, what is your view of the after-death experience?

After this death we are in the astral world, which is still a world of form. We break out of our physical bottle only to awaken inside the astral bottle. Later when we evolve out of the astral, we will be in the causal world, the causal bottle of form. All these are dualistic worlds of form.

This physical world is really about limitations. Many of us, as we age, feel more and more limitation. We have pains. We have less and less mobility. This is to help us let go of this world. It has too much limitation for us. And the body is not who we are.

36 Rabbi Aryeh/ Deep Safety

In Jerusalem lived a modern tzaddik, Reb Aryeh, whose religious practice was deep and full. He slept very little but made it his business to constantly visit people who were in need. Prisons, slums, hospitals – anywhere anybody needed help. And each of these people he was able to see only for a very short time, as so many were in need. People said his touch was almost electric, so soothing. Their lives were eased immeasurably by seeing him face to face. He didn't speak religion to them. He simply connected.

It happened that once when he went to a mental hospital, he sat for awhile with a man who was considered incurable. The doctors had tried everything for him and had concluded there was no hope. This man, after seeing Reb Aryeh, suddenly improved to the point where he was normal and functional. The doctors wondered, how could this be? They called Reb Aryeh and asked, "What did you do?"

Reb Aryeh said he simply listened to him.

But oh, what listening.

To listen, really listen, you let go of your personal stories and you become an attuned receiver for the other person.

Reb Aryeh wasn't doing special healing or magic. He had developed that receptive state, away from the stories, where safety and healing exist. He himself exuded Safety. He radiated his faith in his own Safety, resting in God always, so strongly that he drew forth the innate soul-safety of the insane man. With this sense of safety revealed, the man remembered who he really was.

When we can step back from our own story, we find a place of deep safety. No matter what is happening to us, this safe place is always with us. This is our larger soul.

Our soul comes into this life and looks through our little eyes, hears through our little ears. It is easy for us to believe that what we see and hear on this plane is important, but really it's only the tiniest fraction of our Real Life, of Who we Really Are.

We always have this Safety within us, no matter who we are.

Our story is captivating, though. The difficult part of our life entrances us. And if we get past that most bothersome story, the ego grabs a new one, have you noticed? The ego wants drama. It's almost sick, that way.

Swami Rama told a story about an elderly woman who was dying. All seven of her sons were doctors. Every son did all he could to keep her alive. But she knew it was time for her to go. In fact she told Swami Rama that when she used her life-long mantra, she could see the freedom that lay ahead for her. Her relief was in sight, and she wanted to go straight there into the deepest safety.

Her son would say, "Don't go, don't you love me?"

"Of course I love you, but this is my freedom!"

She repeated her mantra so continuously that after her death, they said the mantra was still sounding off the walls. Swami Rama thought the sons were deluded in saying such a thing. But he went to her home, and yes, he could still hear that mantra going on and on in her room.

By the way, safety arises when we can accept our mistakes. What freedom there is in allowing your mistakes. When you're in safety, all your protection falls away. Suddenly you have access to more of your energy than ever.

It's like military spending. We get caught up in defending ourselves, protecting ourselves, and most of our energy is spent for that. But when we can fully relax and be vulnerable, the full amount of energy flows, undefended, unrestricted.

No effort is required. Only letting go.

37 Duality and Lack/ Abraham, Isaac, Jacob

How are the worlds of duality created?

Through introducing the idea of lack. Restriction. Gevurah.

God is All, God is perfection.

Wherever there is lack of anything, there arises duality. Limitation. Form cannot exist without definition and limitation. We may complain about these limitations.

Abraham represents loving-kindness. He traveled far and wide, filling up lack wherever he saw it. He was sensitive to lack even when people showed a confident front for their own defense. They were defended, didn't want to show vulnerability. He could see past that and offer what was needed.

Isaac's name means "He will laugh." Isaac laughs because he can see duality is sheer illusion. When you see this, all you can do is laugh at it. Isaac is Gevurah, the discipline to see that everything is illusion. Isaac did not have to travel. He stayed in the Holy Land his entire life because he could see past illusions.

Sometimes we reach Gevurah when we've simply had enough of our own games. Like Isaac, we finally say, "Enough is enough." We stop investing in the illusions of this world.

Jacob had the wisdom to balance both loving-kindness and discipline. Both Chesed and Gevurah. He could discern when each was required. He reached a balance of both, which is Tiferet.

Our own mind creates lack. Sometimes our problem arises from our imagination. Imagine the worst, and there it is.

Eventually you see you have been fighting a figment of your own imagination.

What irritates us the most in others is the very thing we do not want to see in ourselves.

Acts of loving-kindness, even if it is just to hold your tongue at a difficult moment, are celebrated more in the upper realms than if you'd won the lotto.

38 Stop Efforting, Bask in the Sun/ Meditate on the Crown

The longer we live, we begin to realize we can stop efforting. All our reading and studying and trying new practices, polishing ourselves. What's it all for?

All our small efforts can't even touch, much less control, the Limitless One. We find that everything we receive is a Gift. We can't do anything to enhance it.

You and your efforts are the character in a dream. Your dream character is working so hard, wanting a reward to enjoy in that dream.

But the reward turns out to be that the whole thing is a dream.

We are being nurtured by the Divine the same way a flower is fed by the sun. You know those flowers that turn to face the sun, wherever it is? How wonderful to be like them, gazing at the sun.

But remember, we are given divine support even when we don't face it. It's always there for us, 24/7. The divine sun shining upon us.

The whole point is to sunbathe. Allow your skin to be blessed by the sun. And instead of covering up some skin and getting a tan line, we need to allow all our parts to sunbathe. All those parts we don't want anyone to see about us. It's not necessary to tell anyone about these parts. Sometimes years of therapy accomplishes very little.

But it is necessary to open your own awareness to those parts you tend to hide, even from yourself. Expose all your parts to the sun. Share your warts and all with God. Let all your parts be blessed. Because they are blessed, whether they seem negative or not. God blesses all of your being.

Many traditions speak about meditating with a focus on the top of your head, the crown. Sometimes you may feel something happening there. The crown is like a doorway. It can open to higher energy. Some people even feel that energy. You might like to give your attention to the top of your head and discover what you sense.

In our tradition, the crown is the place where the soul enters the body. It's located at that soft spot on the baby's head. It's also the place where the soul leaves the body, if you're evolved and fortunate.

One time Isaac visited a well-known and revered elder yogi. All the yogi did was tap the top of his own head and nod at Isaac, as if to say, "This is all you need to work on." And we're done.

39 Rabbi Baba Sali/ Humility

Rabbi Baba Sali of Morocco (1889-1984) was so deeply connected, he knew things of the past and future. People would come to him to find out their future.

During a big Purim party at his house, one of his students jumped up with such exuberance, arms outstretched, that he hit the chandelier. It fell down and shattered in a million pieces. Baba Sali was alert to soothe the fellow and told him he shouldn't feel bad about it. He said each bit of broken glass was to release the sins of everybody there, and more all over the world. He also said, "Don't worry, a new chandelier is coming."

Just a little while later there was a knock on the door. Here came someone who had bought a chandelier many months ago as a gift for Baba Sali, but was waiting for the occasion of Purim to give it to him.

Remarkable things happen around these saintly people, these tzaddiks. Yet they are extremely humble, unassuming, and gentle in their ways. They always discount their own abilities, their own worth. They are the first to say, "I am nothing."

When you are given a look into one of the higher worlds, it is so awesome and you are so small that you are thrown into utter humility. Awe does that to you. You don't have to try to be humble. It's obvious. You are nothing.

Paradoxically, when you realize you are nothing, then grace pours through you stronger than ever. You become a better vehicle for the divine. Yet you know you can't do anything to make it happen.

Our acts of kindness in this world cause God to pour rain down through all the worlds. Your kindness has a direct link to God's response. So close are you to God! That's why thousands are always lined up to come to this earth.

Open yourself with true humility. In authentic service. Available for what's needed each moment.

Learn the path of awe and humility.

You are so small.

You are so blessed.

It takes your breath away.

When you enter this awesome place, all you have is your prayer.

40 Servant of God, Child of God

As we evolve we begin to see more synchronicity in our daily life. Coincidences pop up that are so meaningful, we know they are given to us on purpose. For a moment recall these coincidences in your life . . .

The Sages tell us about the differences in attitude between a Servant of God and a Child of God. Both approaches are divine paths.

"Evid" is the servant. This is the righteous person who becomes interested in the law and the divine order of the Universe. It might begin as the desire to be a good citizen. But eventually the servant is simply following the rules out of love for the sweet order of it all. Then the servant is righteous and is called a tzaddik - saintly.

As time goes on such a person naturally feels deeper and deeper gratitude welling up in them for everything they experience each day.

"Banim" are children. The child of God gradually finds they have no guile and no manipulation of others. There is less and less fear, more and more trust that all is well. God provides. They have no worries. No fear. The child of God is not efforting to earn love, either. They are quite simply just like children who know that Father and Mother love them, no matter what they do. They don't have a care in the world. There is no grasping here. No need to grasp.

There was an Indian saint, a very large man, who would walk through town naked. The authorities asked him to quit doing this. He kept on. They put him in jail. After awhile they saw him on the roof. Every time they locked him up, he would somehow appear out on the roof.

They said he was like the cat on the lap of the Divine Mother. He was a child of God.

41 Grace vs. Efforting/ Manna from Heaven

When we wandered in the desert, God filled all our needs. Manna fell from the sky. The Hebrew word for manna is "man" (pronounced "mon"). "Man" actually means "what." The first morning the manna fell, people ran outside and they all said, "Man hoo? - What is it?" So after that they simply called it "what" - "man."

The Sages tell us "man" tasted like whatever you wished for in that moment. It could taste like meat or milk, whatever. Those who were well-aligned with the Divine, those with the most faith, woke up to find the "man" deposited right outside the door of their tent. Those whose faith was not so strong had to go out into the desert to collect it. They had to make an effort.

You can take the Hebrew letters of "Man hoo" and re-form them, with the same numerical value, into "Emunah," which means faith.

Those who have the deepest faith will have all their needs fulfilled effortlessly.

God says, "I will give where I will give." There's no telling who will receive, or when.

Grace is always available, no matter if we feel it or we don't.

From the upper floors of the metaphorical building, the broad view is that we have no control over God's will.

The word of God is the will of God. God's word always manifests. It never doesn't happen. God's will is continuously happening.

We are not separate beings. There is only One Being. Thus there is only one Will.

We may effort away, day in and day out, to fill our desires. Eventually we come to find, as Solomon found, that the fulfillment of desires leads nowhere. All we really want is to be in the state of grace and effortlessness.

Possessions are irrelevant. The rich man and the poor man each can find love and grace wherever they are, no matter their circumstance.

Even one small moment of feeling grace each day is enough.

42 First Night of Hanukkah

This time of year, in the northern hemisphere, including the land of Israel, we have the darkest day of the year. This winter season is all about Gevurah – strictness, coldness, and fear. Gevurah is fear. In a state of fear we feel cold.

This first night of Hanukkah in some ways is the sweetest of the eight nights, for it is tonight that we bring the very first light out of the darkness. We light the first candle.

We are gathered to commemorate a time when 300 cohanim (priests) held off the gigantic army of a nation. The priests' faith and trust in God made it possible for them to vanquish a huge enemy. Our faith and trust is the only thing that can pull us through the darkest of times.

We might speak about two aspects of God: God the omniscient Creator, and God who watches over each of us personally. The more trust we have, the more we can see and feel the many ways God intervenes in our daily life.

When I give charity to someone on the street corner, that action opens gates through all the worlds. I may never realize it. It was just an urge to do something for the person in need who would really appreciate it, and I wouldn't miss that dollar. It was easy to do. Yet its final effect is far-reaching, throughout the worlds.

There are different points of view we can take. Let's call this POV for short. The broadest view is the POV of the all-seeing God. Sometimes we may be able to gain enough distance to see things with such a broad perspective, and have no fear, and realize that everything is always as it should be.

Then we have the personal point of view, PPOV, which is all about our own little life, its stresses and snags. The deeper we go into our PPOV, the more our fear increases. PPOV is all about how the world impinges on me. I wanted this, and I got that. It isn't fair. I have such suffering.

But when I suffer, it's because I have narrowed my view into the PPOV.

Imagine a set of scales. On one pan sits fear. On the other pan sits faith, trust. When fear rises, faith declines, drops down. When faith rises, fear falls away.

Now the older we get, especially if we keep to our PPOV, fear only increases. Not only fear for ourselves but for our loved ones. We fear for all the others around us. We tend to take on more and more fear. All because of our narrow PPOV.

But remember, in your last moment on earth, it's an experience of the sweetest expansion, when you transition. You leave your PPOV behind, with great relief. If you have lived in your tight little bottle of narrow PPOV, then when you open to broad perspective, it feels amazing.

Here we are tonight in the cold, in the dark, in Gevurah. To turn toward warmth and light, we don't need a blazing fire but only one candle.

In our darkest hour of worry and fear, all we need is the slightest faith. We say, "All right, I know I'm in trouble but I also know it's going to be okay." Just that much faith will help turn it around, because God does all the rest for us.

Remember you can choose Faith or Fear.

The light of the candle tonight is a holy light, different than any other light.

Focus on this special flame and remember how you yourself call up your own faith in moments of difficulty.

43 Elisha/ Baba Sali/ Empty Your Vessel

A young widow came to the prophet Elisha and said she was destitute, how could she support her children? Her sons would be enslaved if she couldn't do something, find some livelihood. She reminded him her husband had been a holy man who followed Elisha's teachings well.

Elisha asked what, if anything, she had in her possession.

Only a small flask of oil.

Elisha told her, "Collect as many empty vessels as you can, go into your house, and shut the door. Then pour from your flask into each vessel."

This she did. One vessel after another was filled to the brim with oil. So she had a source of livelihood.

Baba Sali of Morocco, in modern times, did a similar miracle on several occasions. He was always a good host. He wanted to feed all who came to his home, and sometimes there were hundreds of guests. One such day he asked his assistant, the Gabi (number one student) to pour wine for the two hundred gathered there.

"But Master," said the Gabi, "look, the wine is almost gone." Only about two inches of wine remained in the bottle.

Baba Sali then wrapped a towel around the bottle, and told the Gabi, "Just keep pouring, and don't worry." That is, keep the faith and trust. That bottle kept pouring all day long.

In both of these stories, there are at least two points to remember.

The first point is that we need to have an empty vessel in order to truly receive anything. This is the darkest time of year and a time when we urgently need light. But first we empty ourselves of all preconceived notions and allow the Divine to enter, in whatever form It takes. Without an empty vessel we can perceive nothing.

The second point is that modesty is of primary importance when God lowers the veil between worlds and performs such miracles that go beyond Natural Law. Shut the door. Don't gather witnesses. Don't shout about it to your neighbors. Cover the bottle with the towel.

God hides behind the veil and lifts it from time to time.

You are but a dream in God's mind. When you realize this, it's a sweeter awakening than you might expect.

Unless you still want to be the "little you."

If you waken to the greater reality, it's like a character in a story suddenly wakes up to discover they are only a figment of imagination. They are nothing.

But to awaken to God and become as nothing is the greatest thing you've ever tasted.

44 You Are Never Alone/ Divine Help in Three Stories

In this week's parsha we see that despite all he had been through, Yosef (Joseph) was cheerful. His brothers had sold him into slavery. He was unjustly thrown into prison. He easily could have called himself a victim, but he didn't. Even the prison guard could see there was something special about him. Things went well for him. God was with him. And Yosef could interpret dreams. So it was that he eventually became Pharaoh's right-hand man.

You see, no matter how dark and hopeless things appeared, he knew God was with him every moment. His faith and trust did not falter.

If you forget everything else you hear, remember:

You are never alone. God is with you always.

Here's a story about a friend of mine. This friend eventually became a rabbi, married, and had a large family but hardly any income. One time they prepared to celebrate one of his son's birthdays. They had invited lots of people, friends and relatives, and friends of the children, to come and celebrate. Yet they had nothing ready for the party, and not a penny in the house.

On the birthday morning, the wife woke up all upset, because they were expecting all these people to come, but they had no preparations, not even gifts for their son. She wanted her husband to go to the garage and find something to sell, so they would be able to host this party.

He said, "I'm sorry, but I promised to coach Little League this morning, and I don't want to disappoint the boys."

Off he went to Little League. When he returned, he expected to find her even more upset. But when he opened the door, both she and her eldest daughter were beaming with happiness. What happened? Their youngest child, a girl, was toddling around the house, just learning to walk, hanging onto the furniture. She had put her hand into the VCR and got it stuck. The eldest daughter went to help her, to hold up the VCR flap and extricate her hand. When the little one pulled her hand out, she was grasping a hundred-dollar bill. They took this and bought all the party things.

This story shows us a person who can focus on the Divine strongly, burning up for God and sacrificing worldly concerns. There God answers, dispelling natural law in support of the faithful person.

One of my best teachers, said Isaac, was a woman who would come regularly to our group for learning. She'd had polio, and she used crutches, yet she showed up continually at every event where Isaac was speaking. She always glowed with spiritual joy. In fact she would "dance" with her arms as she sat still, and this would get on some people's nerves.

She could see God everywhere she looked. She had never lost that childhood ability for deep joy, the ability to really see God in everything that crossed her path.

She and her family were refugees who came to Israel after the Holocaust. They lived in a refugee camp for years. She contracted polio and had 36 surgeries, none of which helped her legs, but she was given leg braces for support. Her family made a little cart for her to be pulled behind a donkey for some years.

As a child she was a bright student, yet she would cut classes to go out into the meadow to just pray and be with God. She lived in such deep appreciation of everything in her life, such a joyful connection with God.

She had studied with a Buddhist master who used her as an example to the other students. He would point to her joyful face and tell them, "This is what you should be like." She had to leave the group because she was singled out, and didn't want that.

She would tell Isaac, "Don't make an idol out of me, because idols have to be smashed, and I've already been smashed once." And, "Don't inflate my ego. Are you trying to take me away from my connection with God?"

Isaac asked who were her teachers. She said, "Have you heard of Grandma Helen?" Grandma Helen was her neighbor in the refugee camp, who would come over and tell stories to her. Helen was an agile and able-bodied woman.

When Helen had been in the concentration camp, she would escape at night, go into the town's garbage, collecting potato peelings and such, and then return to the camp to feed the sick and the starving. It was amazing she could escape, much less escape so often. Even more amazing that she would return and serve in this way.

But when a person is given such a gift, like her gift in knowing how to escape, you just have to realize this gift is not meant for yourself alone, but as a way to serve others.

So the woman with polio said Grandma Helen taught her how to whittle down her ego.

Diminishing the ego is like letting air out of a balloon, little by little. The balloon keeps shrinking. Eventually all the air is gone, yet the balloon remains, as a location through which God can work.

Today the main thing to remember is, you are never alone. Despite any catastrophe or fear, remember, you have constant divine help. You are not alone.

45 Pipeline to All Worlds/ Align Thought, Speech, Action

There are many angels in the astral realm and fewer angels in the realm above that. But we, as humans, contain particles of every world, even the worlds above them. The uppermost angels have a vast perspective, but we humans have the possibility to touch even the realms above them, because we have those upper-world particles in us.

When we align ourselves, we have the potential of connecting all worlds above us, through us. It is like opening a pipeline from the highest to the lowest, which is earth. In that pipeline, all valves must be open to allow the flow to come all the way down to us.

How do we align?

The Baal Shem Tov taught his students to align thought, speech, and action.

For us this means first calming our mind. Releasing thoughts. In meditation.

Next we give attention to our breath, to calm down speech. You know we carry speech inside our head. That mind chatter. We use the breath-focus to reduce any attention on that inner chatter. Let speech fall away, dissolve.

Third, we take the action of stillness. We make our body quiet and relaxed.

These are the three valves in our pipeline.

We open these valves to allow divine flow to come all the way down to us.

If you can reach this state, you will feel the connection. Abundant grace pours into you. Usually all questions disappear. You are in the Place. You need nothing. Everything is Here. If you do have a prayer to offer, it rises with your heart, with your full attention, with your presence.

When people say a rote prayer automatically, they shut off the valve of the pipeline, and the flow doesn't pour.

Simply sit and pay attention to all the sounds around you. Let all of them in, because each is a part of yourself. Let yourself be nothing. Can your ego let go and be nothing?

All of life, and all sound, can be a symphony. There may be some notes you consider to be your "self." But you can find a way to let go of those notes and listen to the whole at once.

Hear the whole symphony rather than only what you consider your part.

Let the listener disappear into the symphony.

46 Narrow View, Broad View

Have you ever played with a telescope? How does it enlarge the moon? It narrows the view, which enlarges one item. You block out all the rest of the sky and focus only on the moon. It becomes so much larger.

This narrowed focus works well for examining and studying things. But narrow view also plays a big role in our desire and fear. We narrow our focus and see only our object of desire or fear. We lose the big perspective of the whole sky and all the wonderful things in our life. We narrow the view.

Our attention to desire or fear is magnetic. Desire and fear tend to grab us strongly. We go narrow, zooming in to that desire or fear, shutting out everything else.

In his teen years, Isaac experienced spontaneous rushes of energy up his spine. He had no knowledge of what this meant. It seemed frightening. One night he was rolling over and rolled right up out of his body. He stood there beside the bed, watching himself sleep. There was a sense of profound calm. It felt good. He had a desire to explore the rest of the house this way, but he wasn't sure how to move. He looked at the door, and his desire to go there – his attention – drew him toward the door. Suddenly he felt afraid he might collide with the door. Rather than slowing down, his fear magnetized him all the faster toward the door.

This is an example of how our attention to desire or fear makes us zoom in and go narrow.

We are all being dreamed by our Creator.

When you dream at night, at the end of your dream, the characters fall away, they dissolve, as if they die. Is their death important to you? No. After all, it's a dream. They come and go, just as we come and go in the great scheme of things.

God is One, just as our prayer says. All is One. I am you and you are me. There is no "me."

I think I am me because I put a rubber band around a group of sensations and I call this bundle "me" – my sensations.

When the mystics connect with the Divine and become One with all, they break that rubber band.

You might fear that if you did this, you would lose control of your sensations or the ability to be aware. But you don't lose anything. You receive awareness of all. You go into the broader perspective. You see the whole sky.

You become non-local. You don't have a specific location anymore. The non-local is all here, all the time.

Your awareness is your telescope. Awareness and attention bring you to broad view or narrow view. We tend to live daily life in narrow view. Your awareness narrows down to be "you" and shuts out the broad perspective. This is me, and everything else is not-me. Such is our mindset. Such is our typical telescope focus. Such is our habit of attention.

Now go into meditation for a moment. Remember your streams of sensation – of seeing, hearing, feeling. They are streams because they are always moving. Something new is constantly arising in these streams of sensation.

Can you feel each of these streams flowing by, without calling these sensations yours?

A sensation flows by but does not belong to you personally. You feel it as energy flowing within the One, the All. You hear sound rise and fall, part of the All. You are the All.

Just watch the streams.

Break the rubber band of your bundle.

BE all sensations everywhere.

47 Something about the Sefirot

Isaac began with a little clarification of the sefirot, the emanations or attributes through which the Infinite reveals Itself through us. Each of us have these sefirot. Yehudah fills the central column, the energetic column, of the body.

At Malkhut, the base of our spine, sit both Yehudah and David. Malkhut is kingship, and both of these were kings. Yehudah was the ancestor of David.

At the heart, the quality of Tiferet (beauty, balance) is portrayed by both Yakov and Israel. Yakov is the actual heart quality. Israel carries the energy up from the heart, up through the crown.

Tiferet is the sun around which all the other sefirot rotate like planets. Some sages also go into the "angular aspects" which are the twelve lines between all the sefirot. These represent the twelve tribes. So we see Yehudah exists throughout the whole system.

The distance between heart and crown, or between Yakov and Israel, is the larger part of the central column.

Yosef (Joseph) correlates to second chakra, below the navel, low on the central column. Yosef has to do with the mirror of life. The vibrations or attitudes we send out return to us, like we're looking into a mirror. We find that our trust in God benefits our life. Everything worked in Yosef's life, in his mirror, because his faith was so great. His brothers sold him into slavery, but his place in life improved, because of his strong faith. And yet his faith failed him slightly when he asked pharaoh's butler to mention his name to pharaoh. He was still in prison for two more years after that. The stricter sages say this is because he lost faith in his rapid mirror. But from the upper perspectives there is no such idea of punishment.

Tiferet is beauty. Tiferet and Emet, truth, are one and the same, say the sages. When the human heart opens, it's a milestone. You see beauty everywhere you look. Suddenly even the ordinary cement sidewalk appears breathtakingly beautiful to you.

Beauty is really a matter of our reception. It is in the eye of the beholder, as we've heard before. Even something previously dull and ugly can become beautiful in your eyes.

Question: What can we do when our mind is so busy it won't even settle down for meditation?

Havayah, which is God as Unity, is like the ocean. Elokim (Elohim), which is God as Duality, is the waves. The big waves represent our waking state, our action in the world. Medium waves are the dreaming state. Small waves represent our sleeping state. It is possible to be in all these states at once.

In meditation just allow the waves to rise and fall. Big waves, distractions, small waves - it doesn't matter. All of it is the ocean.

48 Carry Happiness Within/ Dispel Your Clouds

After all the singing and the sweetness of meditation, our whole group sat in a daze, in total comfort. With a big smile Isaac asked if there were any questions.

"They sit with their crowns in their heads," we quoted from Maimonides.

"Exactly," he beamed.

Question: Please clarify how we carry happiness within.

At first we think objects bring us happiness. Whether we focus on a fine car, a home, or knowledge, an education, a career, a social cause - these, we think, are avenues to happiness. We work to obtain such things.

But eventually we find happiness is not dependant on any particular thing at all.

Inner happiness is intrinsic to you. It is who you are. Underneath everything, happiness runs through you. It's natural to you, and it never really goes away. At your core, you are filled with divine light. God lives through you.

But your stories and your disappointments are like clouds covering up the light within. The mind is constantly telling stories. Your heart may be happy, but the mind crops up. Things to worry about.

The biggest hook catches the fish, and your attention follows. So the mind pays attention to the clouds. It seems as if the light is all covered up. The mind buys that story of darkness.

We tend to latch onto our stories because a story makes us important in some way. We can tell others about the trouble. But repeating the trouble just makes more clouds for us, covering up our inner light.

Rabbi Nachman used to speak about "a few good points" in every person. When we are stuck in sadness, in clouds, we can use those few good points as a foundation to rebuild ourselves.

You know how this works. You have experienced it. A glimmer of hope encourages us and leads us toward happiness.

That inner hope lives inside us always, unless we cover it up so much that we can't see it. And when hope feels absolutely gone, there is death. The death of hope.

This week, said Isaac, he had an experience while he was driving along. It was a very subtle feeling of discontent. He noticed it in a brand new way. It felt like someone else was talking to him, focusing on some problem. It was as if he had unknowingly tuned his radio dial to K-SAD. But he saw it, heard it.

Seeing it is the first step to detaching from it. Prior to seeing it, you are one with it. You don't notice it. It runs your life, and you're used to it. It runs automatically. But when your inner witness becomes stronger, you see more and more your own behavior.

It's so easy to get caught in the drama of your own life. It's like some tragedy you might see on the news. The newsman hangs out and keeps interviewing one person after another about how tragic this was, and they show the same film clips again and again. You can't even leave the room because you're riveted to the tragedy. You're scaring yourself and you can't pull away. If anybody else walks into your room, you'll tell them all about it. Your fear directs your attention.

And you feel you must know all the news so that somehow you'll have a handle on all the danger out there. You'll be well-informed. Because all the story-tellers know life is dangerous, after all.

The story-tellers think that those who don't listen to the stories are fools.

The Baal Shem Tov said that the only Yetzir Hara, the only evil inclination, is our tendency to be sad or afraid, to cover up the light.

Light is what we are really made of.

We can dispel our own clouds, layer by layer, to reveal more of the light that has been there all along. We must begin where we are, notice our mood.

When you are under those clouds, what is your truth? Can you speak your truth?

"Here I am, upset by this same thing again." Did you know, speaking your truth aloud increases connection through all realms? You will be heard and assisted.

Speaking our truth helps us dispel our clouds.

This is not your life, as you might think it is. This is God exploring every nook and cranny of the world through you.

Your life is not your life. It is God pouring through you. So your innermost being truly is light and happiness.

The more you allow your attention to be on hope, happiness, and light, the more you notice wonderful things around you. But it becomes so much more than that.

You can find yourself going deeper and deeper into happiness, because its depth is never-ending.

You may find that every sunrise, every bird, every leaf becomes almost painfully beautiful to you.

49 Freedom/ See Beyond Unconscious Behavior/ Marriage

We live in duality. Although we want evolution and perfection, it is not going to happen here.

The goal is to live in duality without suffering.

What if you could reach the place where you see that your life doesn't always follow natural law? What if, from time to time, you notice the Divine Hand arranging things, so to speak? What if more uncanny synchronicities pop up for you?

If we raise our awareness and develop our trust, we can see this.

When we first notice this happening, we might react with fear.

The sages say Fear is a gateway onto the path. Fear gets your attention. Fear changes your behavior.

Each of us is like a little chick pick-pick-pecking at our shell to get out of it. We keep pecking away. When the shell drops off, there is a moment of fear and amazement as our old world disappears and there's a whole new place here.

Eventually we begin again picking and pecking at our world, at our new shell. We never stop pecking and we never finish dropping the infinite shells that contain us, in duality.

God is ever-increasing freedom.

Who has free will? From the top floor of our metaphorical building, we see that only God has free will, to do whatever It wants.

The more freedom we experience, the closer we are to God. On our path we will find more and more freedom.

Comment: This week I found freedom when I uncovered some chronic negative self-talk.

Good, congratulations. Healing follows Consciousness. Wherever we can throw more light, more awareness, then healing flows in.

Question: How can I reframe the politics at work and the undesirable aspects of any situation?

Our unconscious behavior and reactions arise as if we are dreaming them. You don't have to be in your bed to dream. We often live a dream and react to situations automatically.

We carry around expectations and burdens about the politics at work. How can we possibly take a step back and see an old situation freshly?

First we have to let go. Meditation helps. Let the Witness look at the situation. Take a step back. We need to re-contextualize and reframe the situation. What are the positive aspects within it? What is good about this circumstance? Reframe it.

Then we can see past our own dream, our own triggers, our automatic reactions.

Question: What about trying to see freshly in a marriage?

In marriage you find yourself dividing into polarities – one partner versus the other partner. Sometimes the partners seem opposed. But this is part of their dream. If they can see through their dream, if they can see their current situation in a new context, see with the eyes of the Witness, then they can come together with a fresh awareness.

Their situation changes. They look at it with fresh eyes. Then they are able to grow with it. They learn a new appreciation. They wake up on this particular issue.

They can then come together, until the next time they fall into an unconscious dream state.

Those who don't find a new context and renew their relationship will fall into a stale way of being together, where everything is automatic and not alive anymore.

In Hebrew, the word for marriage is holiness. Marriage is a vehicle for holiness.

It's difficult. Yet if you manage to live it with awareness, it leads to holiness.

This isn't the Hollywood version of romantic love. We don't recommend Hollywood love. Look at the marriages of the Hollywood writers and actors. You wouldn't want to follow the illusions they have created for the movies.

Question: So what is the purpose of Hollywood?

To create joy. To allow people to relax and find more joy. To let people escape into a story different from their own, so they can look at their own life anew.

Comment: You have spoken about how we create our own story. You've said when we try to lift our perspective on the multi-storied building, we need to drop our story. And the Baal Shem Tov used stories all the time.

Yes, the Baal Shem used his stories to spread joy. In a joyful state people can see more clearly.

Let's go back to our metaphor of the pool. Imagine there's a secret word written on the bottom of the pool. The vibrations of anger, fear, and lust are chaotic vibrations. They make choppy waves. You can't see through them. You can't even see that there is a word written under there.

But the vibrations of peace, joy, happiness – these are finer and calmer vibrations. These are calm waters. In these waters you have clear vision to see the word of truth at the bottom of the pool.

50 Created New Every Moment/ Horizontal and Vertical

Scientists looked at the brain activity of monks who had been meditating for many years compared to normal brains.

In a normal non-meditating brain, when we experience a brand-new stimulus, there's a big brain wave. As life goes on and we see that stimulus again, the brain produces less reaction, less of a wave. Through time the reaction dwindles, until that stimulus may go unnoticed. It becomes background.

However the long-meditating monks have a big brain wave in response to the exact same stimulus again and again. Their brain reacts as if every time is brand-new and equally interesting.

This points to the way our Sages tell us that the world is actually created new every moment. These monks can experience life that way. No matter how many times they have seen what appears to be the same thing, they still see it freshly the next time.

In our earthly lives, we are immersed in the horizontal world. Here we consider the present moment as a bridge between our past and our future. We stand here and say we understand our life as a product of our past.

But in actuality we are created new every moment.

In the vertical world, "now" – this moment – is everything. Your vertical connection is your very Life, your life force. Creation comes through this present moment.

The horizontal world is all about our story, our job, our goals, where we've been and where we're going.

If we take time to just sit and be present, the people of the horizontal world think we're crazy. They say, "You're not doing anything." But truly that vertical connection is life itself.

Watch in meditation how often your horizontal world keeps inviting you back into the elements of your story. This is different for everyone. Notice how it is for you. Notice what kinds of invitations your mind gives you.

Also in your meditation, listen to everything and experience every sensation as if it is brand new, just born now, never happened before. Because it hasn't.

Every bit is created new right now.

51 Right Brain/ Wordless Wisdom/ Discernment

We have an innate balance between our right brain and our left brain.

The right brain has a sense of union with all it sees. It identifies with everything and perceives no boundaries.

The left brain uses tight boundaries, definitions, words to encapsulate each thing in its separate place.

When we get stressed we tend to move deep into left brain, our logical verbal side. We talk to ourselves, in our head, in a frantic way. This makes everything worse. Lots of chatter, lots of debate, and no resolution.

One way out of this, in keeping with the verbal left brain, is to use holy words of wisdom such as prayer. Even traditional prayers. Use what you have, words, to move into a more peaceful state.

Then your metaphorical pendulum will swing back toward the right brain and achieve balance again.

Question: Are affirmations also considered holy words of wisdom? For example, "I can, I will, I'm able."

Words of prayer will actually take us from stress to a place of less thought, where the stress just falls away. But an affirmation is not quite the same as these holy words of wisdom. Affirmations are good, and they help to heal the ego, which is quite worthwhile.

However the pendulum-shift into right brain has to do with moving into a non-local space. If we were using only our right brain, we would feel as if our body is just part of the scenery. We would feel that we are one big field of energy, where all objects melt into each other without boundaries. We would see no differentiation between ourselves and others.

I would know that I am you, and you are me. In this place, there are no words. Wisdom takes us to a place of no words.

Here we sit in meditation, and to look at us, you might think we were all quiet inside, but we are not. We are all chattering away. If we're lucky we might have a couple tiny gaps between our own clouds, where the sun can peek through. We might get a little taste of wordless wisdom.

In the Torah it says "Wisdom is given to the wise." This doesn't seem fair. After all, the wise are already wise. Wisdom should be given to the ignorant, who really need it.

But upon deeper investigation we find that only the wise are able to create a gap of quiet, a space where the sunshine can pour in.

Light is always ready to pour into us. But if we can't make space for it, we won't experience wordless wisdom.

If we do make space inside ourselves, we may feel or see an abundance of light.

Our Teachers tell us not to chase these lights, because if and when we receive a taste, our ego suddenly pops up with words, "Wow, look at this," and attempts to describe it. Those very words obliterate the gap created by wordlessness. Then we're back in left brain.

This right-brain non-local undifferentiated sense of Unity has been felt by people in all cultures. Religious people might call it God and attach images and personifications to it. Non-religious people – who knows what they might call it.

But we all have a right brain, and it's so close. It's right here. Available. Inside and out.

We're not trying to always be diffuse and right-brained. We simply want to find it in meditation.

Question: Is there benefit in "keeping the Sabbath" in the strict old ways handed down by the sages, compared to lightening up and doing whatever feels better?

Hundreds of years ago, the Roman Church declared it heresy to believe the world was round. They kept the world flat. If you resisted, they would put you to death. If you didn't argue, you could live and be safe. If you noticed the earth's roundness, how could you squash your own truth? How could you keep your integrity? Not to say that you should speak out and invite your own death just for the sake of your integrity.

In the same way, you may feel the strict old ways of keeping the Sabbath are outmoded now. Maybe they are. Okay, but how can we reject our forefathers? They handed down our traditions with great care and thought for us. Each is designed to assist our divine connection. Why not follow traditions?

It comes down to you, thinking for yourself, discerning how you can best honor the Sabbath. The main point is to take time to return attention to your Creator.

When you look at any religion, you are bound to find something that doesn't match up with your own truth. If you find one doubt, you may be left with more doubts.

In an ultra-conservative religious school, a child was sent home for wearing a T-shirt with a dinosaur on it, because the conservatives said there were no such things as dinosaurs. For them the earth was only 5700 years old, so this kid was spreading falsehood.

You know Abraham broke with his tradition. The Talmud tells us that even at a very young age, Abraham knew about Hashem, the One. His father ran a store selling idols, which people worshipped as gods. Abraham smashed every idol. He said, "I don't believe any of this and I'm leaving." Abraham was the first iconoclast.

"Everybody should think for themselves," said Isaac. He considers himself a chef offering dishes from many traditions. Take what you like. Leave what you don't like. It's on your shoulders to discern your truth. We need to grow big shoulders.

Separating from our traditions is a bit like separating from our parents. We start out as children seeing our parents as all powerful. Like it or not. Much of it we don't like. Later we find that our parents did the best they could, good and bad. In the end we see that they are just people. We accept them as people.

Question: Please clarify the line "I am a jealous God."

In reading this on the surface, it might look as if there were competition between gods, but we know there is only One. The deeper meaning here is when we choose to adore something that isn't God, we feel as if God has pulled away from us. It is painful when we make such a choice.

But we are the one turning away, enticed in other directions. God never turns away from us.

52 Build Spiritual Energy/ Become the Divine Flute

We want to choose our actions wisely, to balance the economy of the soul. We want to build our spiritual energy in a steady way.

If you can learn to hold more and more spiritual energy, without wasting or releasing it, the gradual pressure of this energy will bring you to a new spiritual level.

In the field of thought, worry dissipates your energy. Worry is good for nothing but wasting energy.

In the area of speech, we find "lashon hara" – slander. Even if you are saying something amusing, you will find that after speaking slander, you feel bad. Your energy is lower. You have wasted your energy through your speech.

The sages speak about holy speech versus wasteful speech. With holy speech, you do not speak at all unless it is to offer wisdom.

In our lives it's difficult to attain this ideal of silence except to express wisdom.

The elders of Jerusalem are a handful of men who come close to this degree of saintliness. I was blessed to meet one man in particular who almost never opened his mouth. But when he did, it was only to say something wise. If this man lived amongst us, we might see him as unsocial, an ascetic. But in his world, his achievement of tranquility was admired.

The practice of containing and building up spiritual energy will heal and strengthen the nervous system. This is necessary before one can expand to the higher levels of spirituality.

Our Eastern brothers and sisters see this spiritual energy as going right up the spine. It is not exactly in the spine, but in a non-physical location along the spine. You remember seeing pictures of Krishna playing the flute – and they always seem to give him an English-style flute held off to the side, which isn't helpful to this metaphor. Krishna is actually playing a spinal flute, held straight down in front of him, like a recorder style of flute.

So this divine flute is in fact the column of your spiritual energy. You learn to keep your finger on the holes, to contain the energy, in order that God can play His music through you. Each hole in the flute correlates to one of our energy centers, the chakras, which are located in a row up the spine.

The first hole, the first opportunity for leakage, is often about money and fear. This is the root chakra. Your survival. Sometimes it's about anger. But usually the leak here relates to money mismanagement or fear. A good student needs to put a lid on this, learn to keep your finger on that hole, and let the energy rise. Don't fritter it away with fear. This means you take a practical approach to managing your resources, your livelihood. You gain some measure of physical safety, security. You diminish worries and fears.

The second hole, or the second opportunity for leakage, is sexuality and pleasure at the second chakra. Pleasure is a good thing, but you learn to indulge appropriately. In the Jewish tradition there are appropriate ways to express sexuality, and that would be with your spouse on Shabbos. The sages would indulge only on Shabbos. One of the strengths of the Jewish faith is that it incorporates our daily activities and sanctifies them. You use your daily activities as reminders of holiness.

When you learn to contain this spiritual energy and keep your fingers on the holes of your flute, you may find tremendous pressure building. It may surprise you.

Our society is very harsh on holy men who are caught in sexual misdeeds. Most people do not understand the tremendous amount of pressure that built up in them, and how much they endured before they acted on it. We can't even imagine what that is like. At some point their morals were weak, and weren't a match for the energy. This is why ethics and morals are taught over and over again, no matter how evolved the sage is. Because the pressure of that energy is so strong.

The reason some religious people practice celibacy is to rise to new spiritual levels. It's not that they disdain sexuality. They are conserving energy for spiritual expansion.

53 Suffering and Equanimity

Question: Why does God paint His picture of the world with so much suffering in it?

Isaac replied, "Would you rent a movie without any suffering in it?" Even a love story has suffering. If a movie had no suffering at all, it would be too bland. Imagine, the character has a good time – they get up, brush their teeth, go to work, all is well, come home, "Hi Honey how was your day" - nothing happened.

Why would you want to have an adventure? Because you want to be on the edge, you want to allow the unexpected to happen. It's the lure of the unknown. The unknown appeals to us. With the unknown, suffering comes too.

Our world of duality naturally is composed of polarities - best and worst, light and dark. Feeling good or bad. The interplay and contrast not only makes it interesting, but it helps us learn what we came to learn.

The goal of a sage is to treat suffering and pleasure the same. Reb Zusya said - It doesn't matter to me whether God puts me in heaven or hell, because God is with me and that's all I want. That's all I need.

Baba Sali of Morocco asked his assistant to bury him naked in the snow, so he could fully experience the nature of "cold." He didn't do it to make himself suffer. He wanted to feel it without any suffering.

When Isaac began studying with the sages at the yeshiva in Jerusalem, he watched how easily they walked into the mikvah ritual baths. There were two mikvahs. One was as hot as a lobster pot. The other was icy cold. These sages, who had been doing this all their life, were able to enter these waters without hesitation. Isaac figured he could do it too. He tested the hot one with his big toe, and it was all he could do not to scream in agony.

Rabbi Akiva, a sage of the second century, had traveled to the upper realms. He was the only one ever to go there in peace and return in peace. Later he was walking down a road with two other rabbis, and they came upon a corpse. The two rabbis were repulsed by the sight and smell. But Rabbi Akiva said, "What beautiful teeth he has."

That's equanimity. That's balance.

The mind can't direct this kind of balance. It's not something to figure out. It's something that arises. It's a gift. It's like the way you ride a bicycle and balance naturally on it. If you think too hard, you can't do it. But if you allow the motion and the counter-balancing to simply come through, it works.

There's a central column of equanimity inside you. It's an inner balance you can hold, if you're attentive to it.

Here on earth you are in a dualistic world. Every topic is like a stick with two poles. One end attracts us, the other repels us. Both affect us. We tend to split ourselves to the two ends of these polarities.

Consider the energy centers in the body, the chakras and sefirot which also represent our levels of development. The lowest earliest level begins with basic survival at our tailbone. After you master your survival issues, you move upward to deal with the next level of maturity.

But here's the thing. Each level of your development carries the challenge of handling polarities and finding your balance between both extremes. On the level of survival, for instance, you face possible failure to thrive versus thriving to excess, into greed, gluttony, overload. We want to find our balance between those polarities.

Choose the middle way, the middle position of equanimity at the central column.

When you split into polarities at any level – when you go into fear and desire, love and hate -- that is the very point when your movie begins. Illusion begins. Duality sucks you into illusion.

When you heal at that level, when you hold your middle position, then you have the opportunity to see if you can do it at the next level.

When you find true balance you can transcend the suffering on this plane. No matter what your movie shows you, you know it's an illusion. With equanimity you take it all in stride.

Roller coaster up, roller coaster down. You don't take it personally. With this mindset, the movie becomes more beautiful, looking like a story that needs to play out.

54 Purim/ Everything Arises Now

Isaac started off telling the Purim story, as everybody chimed in with "Boo" for Haman and "Yay" for Queen Esther and Mordechai. Most of us have heard this story, about how Haman wanted to slay Mordechai and all the Jewish people. But the tables turned, and the villain lost.

A certain 17th-century rabbi stressed how dangerous it was that the villain Haman was joyful. Because when you are joyful, nothing stands in your way. Haman's intentions were against the Jews. His joy could have brought about their deaths.

"Yesh" is all that is, in this physical world. Yesh is "something." Yesh is all that you can know.

"Ayin" is Nothing. Ayin is the unknowable.

Something always arises from Nothing: Yesh arises from Ayin.

Thus everything is always created now, in the moment.

This is the attitude we cultivate on Purim. Everything arises now. I hold no expectations, even though I've seen natural law play out every day. I expect gravity to work. I expect the usual patterns of existence. But on Purim, things turn upside-down. The unexpected pops up. Everything is created new, in the moment.

Purim is the only holiday where you are "commanded" to drink, and even to get drunk, if you like. We wear masks. We become someone else. Purim is the night to break your own rules, whatever they may be. This is the time to lose the distinction between good and evil. Nothing is as it seems. Don't allow your past patterns to inform the future. Because everything arises fresh, right now.

There was a sage rabbi whose wife was very careful about the family provisions, because of course they were always hosting extra guests and students, and the wife wanted to make sure they didn't run out of food for their children and themselves. She was so careful, she put locks on the cupboards, and she kept the keys.

However. No matter how poor you are, the rule is you should eat well on Shabbos. Even if you have almost nothing to eat the rest of the week. You should do your best to eat like a king on Shabbos. There's a dish of noodles called kugel, and it gets its rich taste from schmaltz – which is fat. Actually it's chicken fat.

Well, from time to time, on Shabbos, this rabbi would ask his wife to put more schmaltz in the kugel. He said it was too dry. But she was so careful with her food stores, she just wouldn't put enough schmaltz in it for his taste.

One day when she was deep in prayer, completely transfixed, he crept in and took the cupboard key from her pocket. He found the jar of schmaltz and dumped a huge extra spoonful into the kugel. Then he carefully returned the key to his wife's pocket, as she was still in prayer.

When the Shabbos meal was served, the wife said, "See how we have been blessed by God Himself with such a delicious kugel!"

The rabbi said, "Yes, my Dear, between the strength of your prayers and my good deeds, we have certainly been blessed!"

Huge blessings should descend on you tonight, on Purim. If you can be so humble and simple not to judge anything. Allow everything in yourself. Accept yourself as you are, fully. Allow all possibilities. Just let you be you. Accept every part of you.

55 Choppy Waves/ "I'm sorry, I love you"/ You are Non-local

Isaac said if we forget all his other teachings, remember the main lesson in meditation is simply to release and let go. Release the thoughts that keep you in your ordinary life.

When you are too busy or preoccupied to meditate at home, you may think you are simply delaying meditation until another day. Not only are you delaying it, but in doing so you are strengthening your attachment to your chronic worldly point of view.

It is as if you are looking through a narrow-view microscope at your regular life, seeing a bunch of threads in a napkin. An ordinary criss-cross limited pattern. You think this is reality. This is the whole world. It's not.

If you could pull yourself away from your narrow microscope, you would see the whole napkin. You would see a lot more around you. You would take a broad view.

We want that bigger perspective in meditation. We release our attachment to the microscope of our regular concerns.

As we observe our thoughts and let them go, we are alert to the ones that pull us the most, our desires and fears. These are easy to see.

It is more difficult to release the subtle chronic thoughts that creep in unnoticed. So we need to stay alert and drop each thought that might arise.

Let's consider the image of the pond, where turbulent thoughts make choppy waves. It's turbulent, cloudy, unclear, because there's too much distraction. Where's the clarity? It's confusion. In choppy waves, you don't know which end is up. Subtle intuition is too soft to perceive because it's like a tiny pebble. A pebble thrown into choppy waves won't be noticed. It takes a boulder to make a big enough splash that you will notice.

Someday when you can calm your mind and your pond, you will perceive the pebbles. The pebbles are intuitions, perhaps even divine messages.

Question: Please elaborate on exactly how we can release better, and also how to drop worry. Sometimes when we think we're dropping worry, it only goes deeper underground.

The best way to release is to simply learn to drop the thought right in the middle. Realize this thought is carrying you, and just drop it.

Have you noticed, when you're having an argument, sometimes you will see your defense is thin and weak and even just wrong? But your ego keeps going for it, keeps defending your stance. What if you just dropped it? It's such a sweet relief to simply let it go.

And yes, we do have worries and chronic issues that go underground. We may think we are a kind generous person, until something hits us. That underground stream hits a hole and bubbles up right in front of us. We go into a rage.

Afterward we don't want to admit we were angry. That's not us, we say. That's not who we think we are.

We need to embrace that part of ourselves, too – the angry part. When we're aware of our own anger, it won't surprise us that way. We may be able to express it better next time, rather than to suddenly explode without warning.

We need to allow that sometimes we play the fool. The more foolish you can allow yourself to be, the more child-like and present you can be. That's the humility you want.

We can let go of our past worries and start fresh now. The ex-alcoholic should not keep saying "I'm an alcoholic," because that is in the past. That's a memory now. It doesn't matter what your chronic issue was. You can release it now.

We can step into the present and allow our past memory to be past.

This way each event of our life can arise new. You don't have to let your past color your future.

Recognize that when something hits you the wrong way and sends you into anger, it is because of something you don't like in yourself. The world is your mirror. Everything that bothers you in the outer world is really part of your inner world. That's why it hits you with discomfort.

The kahunas of Hawaii repair the world by saying, "I'm sorry, I love you." They are speaking to the world and to themselves. Everything is us.

But think about it, who are you saying "I'm sorry" to? You're saying it to yourself, to the disowned part of you. "I'm sorry I insulted you. You are God's gift."

To whom are you saying "I love you"? Yourself.

It's been said before, and yet it's primary: learn to love yourself.

Give loving attention to all the parts of you. When you can give yourself this kind of loving attention, to every part, you begin to meld together your conscious mind and your unconscious mind. The two minds come closer and closer together until they are one, and you are then unified. You have full acceptance of all your parts.

God is okay with the heights of Light and Happiness and with the depths of Darkness and Pain. All of it is okay with God. Try to make all of it okay with you.

As you continue on your spiritual journey, it becomes clearer and clearer to you that your inner world plays out in the outer world. This is your mirror. The more often you notice events reflecting your inner state, the faster your mirror. When this first occurs, it's uncanny.

For instance, you wake up aggravated about some pressure you have to face at work. Next, you become a magnet for aggravations. You cut yourself shaving. You spill coffee on your shirt. You have to hurry or you'll be late. But now your car won't start. The battery is dead. Underneath all this, you wonder how you got trapped in this ditch of aggravation. You may notice it began with you. The world mirrors you.

Or on a better day, you wake up feeling good. Let's say your sinuses are clear and you thank God you're healthier than yesterday. You become a magnet for good feelings and clarity. You open the window to a beautiful day, to fragrant flowers. You hear laughter somewhere nearby. The phone rings, and you discover a previously sticky problem got resolved smoothly without your effort. Things get better and better all day. This is your mirror.

Synchronicities pop up in front of your face. It may inspire the fear of God in you. You're telling someone about your favorite plumber, and his truck drives by. Or you're pondering a line of poetry, and the very image in it unfolds in real life. A rose by any other name is suddenly there in front of you on the sidewalk.

Such moments remind us that our inner tone will be mirrored "out there."

This is difficult when we are angry, depressed, fearful, because the world brings us more of the same. "I'm so afraid I will be robbed." Are you? You don't have to be.

You know, to get your attention, your soul will whisper or shout. If you still can't hear, your soul will order off the menu of the Universe to bring events into your life that will make you sit up and listen. Sometimes we need to be hit with a two-by-four, it seems, for us to wake up. Those are tough moments. But we learn.

Realize that the real You is non-local. The larger You is everywhere and everything. You are every atom in the world and out of this world.

You are more a feeling than a thing. You are not your body. You are the bees buzzing in the flowers.

When you really get it that you are nonlocal, then you're not even here. When you really get it, and you pour loving attention on all parts, and you unify the conscious with the unconscious, then you may find yourself indulging in utterly spontaneous actions. You come from a place of calmness, and you suddenly feel moved, not from your agenda, but from Source, to put yourself forth in some situation. You become an agent of the Divine.

But also in this state of being, it may get tricky to discern between quiet contentment and the ego's impulse to withhold and avoid participation. So strengthen your inner Witness, always, for keen discernment.

To clarify: when you give your parts your loving attention, it's not that you are telling your inner child, "You're ugly but I embrace you anyway." Rather this is benevolent loving attention, the same kind of attention God gives you. This is real appreciation for all parts.

Your loving attention is part of the Unity.

The Witness implies watcher and object - witnessing Duality.

Question: Sometimes my inner Witness tells me I'm helping others in order to pump myself up. What's that about?

Yes, sometimes you may help others because it inflates your ego. "Look at me, I'm a great helper and proud of it." Such help may be worse than no help at all. You're so eager to play the role, you get pushy about it. You may push your service on others who don't want it.

When you help from your heart, it is humble. If your help is inappropriate or not wanted, you bow out gracefully.

When helpers are given special gifts, like psychic awareness, there's a danger that they may look around, compare themselves with others, and focus on just how special they are. While preening their ego, they lose sight of their service. When their specialness increases, their service decreases.

Divinely-connected service is humble. Just a human being, responding to what's needed in that moment. No strings attached.

56 Golden Calf/ Errors/ Astral World/ Giving of the Torah

Our discussion began with a lengthy question about the sin of the golden calf. When Moses returns down the mountain and sees the golden calf, he asks Aaron, literally, "Why did you let their sin come out?"

Aaron replies, "You know that's just how they are."

It's as if our sin is part of God's plan. And not only that, God made the golden calf for us. It says Aaron threw the gold into the fire, and the calf appeared.

So is God causing our sin, because God creates everything in existence?

Isaac, smiling at the multi-leveled question, began by reminding us that the word for "sin" in Hebrew is "chet," which means missing the target. "Chet" doesn't have all the negative baggage attached to the word "sin" in English. In Hebrew it simply means, "You didn't shoot straight."

At our basic level of understanding, we have choices, and sometimes we make errors. God allows us free will, which includes missing the mark.

From the lower floors of our metaphorical multi-storied building, our understanding includes the concept of free will. However we know that on the lowest floors, our view is somewhat limited.

From the upper floors there is a broader view. That's where we see that God is running everything, despite our lower-floor opinion on our free will.

When Moses speaks to Aaron, he is talking about Aaron's responsibility to the people. The sages tell us a tzaddik is like a tree trunk. That tree trunk is the conduit that feeds every branch and a multitude of leaves. If any branch is cut off, all the little branches and leaves die too. The tzaddik must stay ever-grounded to his Source and ever-mindful of the many who depend on him. As a tzaddik you are responsible for all those you touch.

In fact a certain rabbi long ago was blamed for the death of a man eaten by a lion, three miles away from his home. People said that should not have happened. Somehow the rabbi wasn't maintaining his vibration. Everyone within a three-mile radius of the rabbi should have lived in safety always.

So when Moses says, "Why did you let their sin come out," he implies that Aaron slipped up. Aaron shrugs it off, tries to wiggle out of it, as we all might do. People are just that way, he says. We miss the mark.

God is not "causing our sin." That's on us. We didn't shoot straight. We try again.

Question: Isaac, tell us more about the differences between this world and the astral world?

In the astral world we have instant manifestation. Whether we are indulging in pleasure or pain, desire or fear, it unfolds immediately for us in the astral world. We can get carried away by an obsession with a particular pleasure. Or locked into a specific pain. We tend to get caught in a loop there. We perpetuate our obsession, whatever it is.

Many religious traditions all over the world speak about Heaven and Hell as being in the astral realm. This reinforces the idea that we can fully indulge our delight or lack of it in the astral world.

Here on earth things don't appear instantly. The reason people line up to come to this world is because this world helps us to break our obsessions. This world has a time lapse between our desired intention and its manifestation. We don't get immediate gratification. We are forced into patience.

Because of this time lapse we can detach from our obsession more easily.

Question: But we are existing in all worlds right now, aren't we? We're there in the astral, doing all that now?

We do exist on all levels, but our focus is here in the physical right now.

In the astral realm we can become ever lost in endless delight. We might attach to that delight and forget about God.

Or we might attach to fear. Fear is most prevalent in this earthly world, but it exists in other worlds too.

In fact the highest form of fear is something beautiful that everyone would want to experience. That highest form is breathless awe.

The lowest form of fear, found most often here in our world, is worry. Worry serves no purpose.

All these worlds are busy with constant change, like a wheel spinning. But no matter how fast the edges spin, the center is always in stillness – like God.

Our sages tell us, God alone exists.

God is alone. God creates everything. And only God is free. In a sense, everyone and everything is a slave to something above it, another world above it, except for God.

God alone.

So you could say God is freedom. Our path is toward ever-increasing freedom. When you say, "I want to be free," you are really saying, "I love God."

At the highest levels of existence, the seraphim, you remember, are being born only for a moment, just long enough to burn up with their love for God and disintegrate back into Him. Then they are reborn, to love God for a moment.

"Oh, wait a minute," Isaac suddenly said. "There's a big argument going on here." (He smiled, listened to the air, and proceeded to explain.)

"So there are two camps. Both are right; they have their place. One camp says it's all about coming so close to God, like the seraphim, in a position of adoring God. That's duality. To love means you are separate. But being separate, you are able to focus your love, able to go on loving.

"The other camp says it's all about Unity, really becoming one with God. Not separate. Merging into One. Disintegrating."

Question: Tell us about the giving of the Torah.

On Mount Sinai that day, both a written Torah and an oral Torah were given by God. The oral Torah was much larger than the written Torah.

The written Torah has four levels to it. The first, P'shat, is the simple story-level. The second level is called Drash and is the moral application of the simple story. The third is called Remez and contains hints and clues for deeper understanding. The fourth level is called Sod, the secret level or the Kabbalah, the mystical understanding.

The larger oral Torah was to be passed down only through the spoken word. It had to be memorized. People would spend their entire lives memorizing it, from their boyhood until they were old men. Many generations were able to do this, to hold that much oral Torah in their heads and share it with the people.

But eventually there came a time when we had less and less capacity to memorize all that. So Judah the Prince, who was the highest sage of his era (born in 135 CE), decreed that we could write down headlines of the oral Torah. These were just lines to prompt the memory for the rest of it. If you read these headlines without any background, they wouldn't make sense to you.

They called these headlines the Mishna. When you change the letters of Mishna around, you get the word Neshama, which is the Hebrew word for the soul at the causal level. Thus the Mishna is the teaching from the causal world.

A few hundred years later, the capacity for memorization decreased even more. At that point they wrote the Gemara, which was the information belonging to each headline of the Mishna. So the Mishna and Gemara together are the Talmud. The Talmud contains many dozens of volumes. Several shelves of books.

57 Stillness/ Wave-life and Still-life

We have so much trouble turning off our thoughts during meditation. It's difficult for us to find that still water of the pond. One renowned Eastern teacher used to tell his students, "Every time you pass by a pond, sit down and meditate." It wasn't that the water had special properties. Rather it was to help them remember that our meditative state and our inner self should be as calm as that still water.

During meditation our thoughts arise like waves in the water. But we do not have to go with those waves. Return to the still water.

Sometimes we try to get into a particular sensation that we think is a "good" meditation. But that is another kind of wave. It is sensation. Not stillness.

As we continue our meditation practice through months and years, we might have special experiences, psychic developments. But these too are waves. They are not the still water. Don't let yourself be distracted by these things. They're just another wave.

The purpose of making regular visits to the still water is to learn that this Stillness underlies everything. We go from our wave-life to our still-life and back to our wave-life. In going back and forth, we come to know, solidly, that our wave-life is an illusion. All the stresses we have, the issues, the thoughts, the stories – all of it is illusion.

It is our steady practice of meditation that brings us this wisdom. Nothing else will help us learn this.

(Isaac continued, but I lost the rest of the words. Listening to his voice, I became more and more tranced and empty-headed. This seemed to happen to everyone. We got steadily saturated with calm.)

Soon Isaac said, "You see? Here it is. This is the place we need to be."

(We had all slowed down into emptiness. Stillness. Couldn't think a thought.)

"Okay," said Isaac. "Go spread this around."

58 Divine Mother/ Passover/ Increased Awareness

After meditation Isaac said he was being provoked to share a story with us.

One day some years ago, he opened Yogananda's autobiography to read at random for inspiration. It opened to the chapter that described a time when Yogananda was a young boy, interacting with his first teacher. This was a school teacher who was very evolved and compassionate. He had received blessing from Rama Krishna. He taught school subjects but he also tried to bring his spiritual knowledge to the children. He was a gentle teacher, never a cross word with anyone, always incredibly patient.

One day young Yogananda went to ask him a question, and the teacher was in meditation. Yogananda tried to get his attention.

The teacher said, "Please young sir, not now - wait a bit, for I am speaking to Divine Mother."

Yogananda was so stricken with this idea, and he suddenly missed his own mother, who had died some years before. He'd had a wonderful bond with his mother and he missed her intensely. He burst into tears of longing right there in front of his teacher, and said, "Please intercede with Divine Mother on my behalf, and ask her to reveal herself to me!"

The teacher was stunned and humble. He felt this request was out of his league. Yet Yogananda was weeping so hard. He said, "I will try to do as you ask."

That evening Yogananda went to a quiet attic room in his home and waited for the appearance of the Divine Mother. At ten o'clock exactly, the room was filled with such a beautiful revelation of the Divine Mother, that Yogananda's life was changed forever by it. He was transported, and his spiritual life began.

The next day when he went to see his teacher, he wanted to test him. He asked, "Did you speak to Divine Mother for me?"

The teacher looked at him and said, "Naughty boy! You know I did!"

When Isaac closed the book that day, he too was filled with longing for the Divine Mother. He had read this chapter many times, and while it was always wonderful, this time it affected him more deeply than ever. He found himself in tears. Using the Indian tradition, he prayed to Divine Mother to show Herself to him. He was begging. His longing flooded him as he prayed. After awhile, he settled down, dried his face, and went downstairs.

His son, ten years old at the time, grabbed him and said, "Abba, Abba, come here. I want to show you something." (Abba means Daddy.)

Out in the backyard gravel a big circle was drawn, and inside it, the symbol for Om, perfectly drawn. Isaac was amazed. "How did this come to be here?"

"I don't know. I just suddenly felt like drawing."

The boy may have seen this symbol somewhere before, and yet it was as if God poured through him in answer to Isaac's plea.

Question: Please tell us something about the upcoming Passover holiday?

Passover is all about freedom. As we have learned, God is truly free. Everything else is in different degrees of slavery, if you will. Our increasing freedom brings us closer and closer to God.

Passover is also about the balance of suffering and joy in our lives. When I eat a spoonful of fresh horseradish that I ground myself, I know how suffering feels. But the Sages tell us, for each spoonful of horseradish, we should drink four glasses of wine. Balance the suffering with plenty of joy. Taste the haroset, the sweet paste of apples, honey, and cinnamon which is also part of the seder plate.

We need to bring an abundance of sweetness into our lives.

When life is difficult, it doesn't help to stay in our darkness and complain. We need to get out, see friends, go to the movies, sing. We need to uplift ourselves. So - four glasses of wine.

The matzah unleavened flatbread is simplicity, of course. It reminds us to simplify our life so everything can flow more easily. We don't need as much as we might think we need. Possessions can become burdens that slow down the flow of life.

We don't need to fix our flaws. Awareness itself is curative. Just being aware of your own behavior, just seeing it, is often enough to correct it. When you see your blind spot, your habitual reaction and how it impacts others, you naturally want to make a better choice.

We accept our traits, positive and negative. We accept our humanity.

I contain both light and dark, giving and taking, aggression and retreat, all these opposites.

When opposites split from each other, they yearn always to get back together. They want to be held, both together. They go together, really, in this duality. You can't have one without the other. Mountain and valley, high and low, the crest and the dip of the wave.

The positive and negative poles of a battery need each other. When you hook them up to each other, the current flows.

The Divine current is always seeking a way to flow.

Question: You say it's enough to see our poor behavior, but isn't forgiveness important?

Yes and no, because the very awareness heals. Underneath everything, we really don't need to fix things. All is in right order. It is our awareness that is growing, our understanding that brings more freedom and peace.

Question: Sometimes the words of the Masters can help us into greater release?

Yes and no. The Masters can point the way, but you need to learn to release on your own. You don't really need a teacher. There is too much reliance on teachers. The best way is to choose your growth for yourself. Learn your way.

Question: As my spiritual journey continues, I find myself sometimes forgetting the daily-life things I used to keep track of.

Yes, and this is not all Alzheimer's. As you evolve, you naturally re-prioritize the things you're really interested in. Your old interests don't match up with your new interests.

Emotion causes us to remember things. If you don't feel as much emotion with certain things, you won't remember them like you used to do. Your priorities have changed. You will be remembering on new topics. You will remember what you really care about.

It is this increased awareness that helps us move from one level of our metaphorical building to the next level. In a way, every bit of increased awareness is more enlightenment.

59 Holy of Holies, The Temple/ New Era/ Unusual Questions

Whether it was traveling in the desert, or built to last like Solomon's Temple, the ancient Temple was always set up the same way. The innermost room was the Holy of Holies, where the Ark of the Covenant was kept. This space was 20 x 20 using a measure of the forearm, from fingertip to elbow.

Every name of God emanated from the Holy of Holies, each name in its own stream, flowing out into the world to fulfill its particular purpose. These streams flowed first through the sanctuary, then through the courtyards, and finally out into every place in the world.

A larger sanctuary encompassed and surrounded the Holy of Holies.

On either side of the doorway to the Holy of Holies sat two important items. On the right side was a special menorah with all of its lamps turned toward its center stem, which is regarded as the face of the menorah. On the left side, a golden table held a loaf of bread. This was to remind everybody of the blessings eternally bestowed.

In the center of this large sanctuary stood a square gold altar, and here only one kind of offering was burned, the highest offering, which was incense. Only the high priest was able to make this offering.

This altar, where the incense was burned, was considered the umbilical cord of the whole world, because this incense connected all human souls to the bliss of the divine flow, or "shefa." In a sense all the bliss of the world was concentrated at this one place, at this altar.

Incense burns down, totally consumed by fire, with virtually nothing left over. In the same way the human soul is consumed by the Divine.

In Solomon's Temple, this altar, the umbilical cord of the world, was placed on the same rock where Abraham almost sacrificed Isaac, which was the same rock where Jacob slept and saw the ladder of angels coming and going to divine realms. So this altar was connecting all realms to the human world. All human souls would receive this blessing of shefa (divine flow) from this very place.

Moving further through the Temple, beyond the large sanctuary, outdoors stood the higher and the lower courtyards. Here the archangels and angels would receive their blessings of shefa. Beyond the courtyards the blessings would spread throughout all the physical world.

Solomon was gifted with special sight to see all these streams of divine energy flowing everywhere. He could choose the best spot for a non-indigenous plant to grow, and it would thrive there. These courtyards were beautiful gardens with wondrous variety.

As we know, said Isaac, angels are born to serve God. When they fulfill their function, they're finished. A human can become like an angel, running to serve God. After their season of being like an angel, the person will become human again, to enter into the deeper sanctuary and receive the greatest blessing, which is for human souls.

In our written records it says the third Temple will be built by God. Yet another passage says it will be built by people. Currently one of our Sages says it will actually be a holographic Temple that will appear, sent by God, and people will fill it in with the physical building. And it will be placed on the same site as Solomon's Temple.

Apart from these traditional mystical teachings, the time is approaching when we may experience a new reality. Consciousness will change, and everything will look different to us. A shift will occur from the old wisdom into the "time of Keter." The crown. We will understand that we are truly extensions of God. God is flowing through us and becoming all that Is. We are simply conduits.

At this point we will fully understand that I am you and you are me. There will be no doubt. It will be undeniable and obvious. Everything has consciousness. Birds, trees, rocks.

We will see God in everybody and everything. We will watch God's will pouring through us, right into every aspect of our lives.

A person needs to be only two things: available and alert. Ready to serve the needs of the moment, whatever they may be.

This kind of readiness is more valuable than intelligence.

Our lives won't change much. Daily life will play out as usual. We'll still have challenges, but our perception will change. Our consciousness will deepen. We'll be watching God pour through, everywhere we look.

There is no telling when this new understanding may arrive. It may take a long time yet. But here in our circle we may feel a little of it. It really depends on people. And this is the sort of teaching that, when you name it, you call it forth.

Question: How will this new perspective play out with our nations and international relations?

Nations will still be unique, offering their own ways of doing things, their unique cultures, but there will be no more wars. You see that everybody is you. You don't kill yourself.

Question: How is it that some people are able to see clearly the past and the future?

All knowledge of the past and the future is playing all the time, like on radio stations. Those who can tune in to the appropriate vibration can find information wherever they need to do so. They turn their radio dial, tune in and listen.

"The Holographic Universe" by Michael Talbot included a chapter where a psychic man from Poland could hold any physical fragment, and a virtual movie would unfold before him. It showed everything that happened with that item, and how the people of the time combed their hair, what they did, and how they lived their lives.

Question: As we count the Omer now, we're counting the days between Passover, the end of slavery, and Shavuot, the giving of the Torah. Would you speak about our current challenge of Gevurah, restriction? How can we look at it in a better way?

Well, for instance, said Isaac, when I went to my car this morning it had a flat tire. Gevurah, restriction, is about adversity. Look at places in your life where you face adversity.

When a challenge comes up, do you explode, rant and rave? Or do you take it in stride, with patience? Adversity is to teach us patience.

We often take offense at others' behavior. But frequently it boils down to the fact that it was my problem, not theirs. This is where Gevurah teaches us.

Question: Is there a tradition in the Torah about seeing physical illness as a metaphor for what is wrong with the spirit, or the emotional body?

Yes, in fact it is said that each of the 613 mitzvot (good deeds) are associated with a different organ of the body or the muscles and sinews. There are 365 negative mitzvot (as in, "don't do this") and 248 positive mitzvot (as in, "do this"). One Rabbi long ago made a catalogue of which mitzvot belonged to which organ. (Rabbi Nachman's Anatomy of the Soul.)

Tradition says each of us must complete these 613 mitzvot, but that's a lot. It can't be achieved in one lifetime. The Sages tell us it takes many lifetimes to accomplish this. Some stories tell of persons who returned here for the sake of finishing one last mitzvah.

Question: Do gemstones actually hold special vibrations that are useful to us?

Yes, they do. From ancient times, the high priest's breastplate held twelve gemstones. Each had a special purpose to bring in particular energies or vibrations.

Are there any other questions? Even something strange or bizarre, it doesn't matter?

Question: I've got bizarre one. Does this tradition say anything about fairies? I mean, the Talmud says there's an angel holding up every blade of grass?

Isaac grinned and replied that the Torah calls all of these things angels. The Torah makes it clear that there is nonphysical help supporting this physical world in every detail. The most important thing to remember is that all of this support is filled with consciousness.

Whatever needs to be done is done with consciousness.

All of it is God's loving attention. Consciousness fills everything.

Question: Along those lines, there are places in the Torah where animals speak. And the Baal Shem Tov even heard rocks speak. Tell us about that?

Yes, many sages have heard rocks speak. Even the rocks in the walls would call to them and tell their stories. When you think about communication as vibration, then hearing rocks or animals becomes understandable.

If you had a thought to convey to a Chinese person but you didn't speak the language, could you convey it? Of course. So when we communicate with animals, it's like that. Vibration is communication in all languages.

The Baal Shem Tov not only freed souls from rocks, but at the end of every Shabbos, he would light up his pipe and free souls that way too. At the end of the fourth Shabbos meal of the day, on Saturday night, he would smoke his pipe. His students asked him about it, and he told them that some souls had extremely little substance, but they were drawn in by the fragrance of his pipe smoke. With his smoke he could help them finish the one small elevation they needed, and convey them to heaven. He was so aware. His perception was acute.

Question: Can we learn to do things like that?

You know, Yogananda in his youth was fascinated by such supernatural things. And his teacher, Sri Yukteswar, made it very clear to him that finding supernatural powers is not finding God. Those are distractions which are not recommended.

Question: Recently I heard you say that rhythm can lift us from sadness?

That's right. I learned that from a certain teacher-sage who was drumming his fingers on the table. Rhythm dispels negativity. When you're feeling down, put on some music. It lifts you. You have seen how a song can bring people together. As long as there's a rhythm, everybody can join in, in whatever way they wish. The rhythm of it makes that possible.

Question: I've been wanting to ask this for years. We never hear anything about Mrs. Baal Shem Tov, or any of the wives of the Sages. We know these women must have been amazing, just because they were married to these men. Is there anything written about any of them?

No, there is very little if anything handed down to us about the wives of the Sages. This is an unfortunate omission. Elijah made it quite clear that our spiritual perception and ability is not at all dependant on our sex, our age, our race, or anything else. Everyone, male and female, is equally able to experience the Divine.

Yet there is a long tradition in our culture of the men rejecting the Divine Feminine. They walled off the women from themselves, both metaphorically and physically, as they divided the space, men from women, in the synagogue. Men did this because they felt women would take them away from spirituality. In other words, men succumbed too easily to their attraction toward women.

Even Devorah, who was the head of a nation – when men came to speak to her, they stayed behind a screen.

This rejection of the Divine Feminine does need to be rectified.

60 Meditate on a Clear Pond/ Untie the Knot/ Handle Anger

Meditation is like looking into a pond to see a clear reflection of your face. Reaching that stillness brings clarity.

Maybe the wind kicks up or throws pebbles into the water. The waves begin. The ripples break up your image into fragments, bits of colors, so you can no longer recognize yourself. And that's the world, too – it exists in so many pieces. Pieces that don't make sense.

Both of these experiences, the still clear pond and the rippling pond, are part of the big picture. One is not better than the other. We can visit each of them.

You will remember, as we've said before, there are only two things to do in meditation.

1) Don't splash – don't make waves with your busy thoughts.

2) Wait patiently for your prior waves, that were already set into motion in the past, to wear themselves out and come to stillness.

Don't expect instant success with this. Even if you learn not to splash, that is, to quiet your thoughts today, you have ripples moving from before. We might consider these ripples your karma.

Meditation is all about releasing. It's not effort. If you're efforting toward stillness, you're on the wrong track. It's an allowing of what exists. You freely and easily allow things to be as they are, at all times.

Yogananda used to call it "lashing the pond" whenever his thoughts disturbed him. Yet he also wrote that sometimes when he walked down the road, suddenly the whole world around him changed. Trees, houses, everything in his sight would be fully absorbed into light. This came upon him with profound joy.

At first it was an unpredictable occurrence for him. But eventually he noticed that this light revealed itself only when he had no mental turbulence within him. When his mind was still and fully at peace, that's when the world shifted into light.

One way of being is not better than the other. These are simply two ways of being. Unity and Duality.

It's just that sometimes, some of us have lived in the waves for so long, we doubt the existence of stillness. We get used to living in the fragmented world, and we think that's all there is.

The dualistic world is more dense. Living there all the time perpetuates our dense nature. We can get stuck in our habits. For instance, we know intellectually that it's not a good idea to respond with anger. But in a dense world, it's easy to keep responding with anger.

When we visit the Stillness, anger makes no sense there at all. There's nobody to be angry at, because we are all One.

It's not that we learn to control our anger in the world. Eventually we just see that choosing anger is not in our best interest. Our anger inhibits our own well-being.

We find that some sages, to reduce their anger, would retreat to caves and forests. They would isolate themselves and simplify the routine of their lives in order to touch the Stillness. But if you were to bring them back to the city, they might react as strongly or stronger than anyone. Their isolation did little to trim their reactivity.

So there is merit in living in the city and attaining modest gains of calmness. The people around us are meant to challenge our behavior and help us resolve our karma.

Even the great masters have had their own karma to deal with. Even the greatest sages have had their physical weakness, emotional conflicts and other ailments.

Our challenges and difficulties are like knots. Any recurring issue in us is like a rope we have bent this way and that, squeezing it around itself like a knot. To unpack and learn from this issue, we need to pull the rope out gradually, first from the most recent part of that big knot. The most recent rage on a recurring confrontation, for instance. In a calmer state, we take time to look at it. Why does this bother me? Why do I react so much? Uncurl that part of the rope.

On its way out, the rope must pass through the same way it came in. Every knot needs to be untied in the same way it was tied.

It takes patience and a strong inner Observer to do this work.

This is the Observer or the Witness we develop through meditation. It's the ability to step back and watch what you do. You gain enough space inside that you're able to observe your own behavior, your standard automatic reaction.

When one of our hair-trigger reactions pops up, we might be able to take a breath and observe it.

Imagine you're on the brink of such a reaction. The pressure builds up inside. It feels so easy to go over the edge and release anger in the old habitual way. The old habit rises strongly, overpowering the very dim idea that you could choose calmness.

And yet, somewhere deep inside, a gentle insight may arise, telling you that you may choose as you wish, but know that if you release anger here, you create a long line of consequence upon consequence. In fact it may lead you into another life, as it were. It takes you into a parallel universe where everything will be different for you. Eventually you will forget you were ever in this universe, this smoother vibration. That can be the power of one choice.

And you can handle this situation yourself, with your meager assortment of tools, or you can let God do it. Give it to God?

What would you do?

61 Develop Awareness in Waking, Dreaming, Deep Sleep

As humans we have three states of experience: waking, dreaming, and deep sleep. If we can learn to live in all three states at the same time, then we have full alignment and true Presence.

We already know how to do each of these things. It's only a matter of bringing them together more often with awareness. Meditation assists in this. Remember, meditation is not a matter of effort. If you say, "I will stop my thoughts now" – that is a matter of control and effort. Instead approach meditation with the attitude you have toward taking a nap. When you want a nap, you choose to let go of problems and just lie down. Let go. Let the nap happen. Witness your calm state of being.

Waking, dreaming, and deep sleep are three states of awareness we go to naturally. Our brain waves change with each state.

Your waking state is this parenthesis of eternity which you call your life. This tiny part is not who you really are. Your larger self gives attention to this parenthesis of time and space. Your larger self squeezes into this spacesuit which you see as you. Your attention to it creates this form. Here I am Isaac, with inherent limitations. I have become Isaac with Isaac's ego, personality, and body, in order to fit into this time and place and way of being.

This is a world of detail and limitation. This waking world is a world of form, so it can be used for building and learning. Your larger self chose to explore some detail here. For instance, if I'm interested in mathematics and all its beauty and wisdom and perfection, then I want to come and spend fifty years studying and playing and building my knowledge of mathematics. Or I want to learn more about relationship, and I spend thirty years building a relationship. One step at a time, and the steps are cumulative. We progress.

We can see also that memory creates this waking world. We expect things to go as they go because of our memory about how they went before. Not just our personal memory but the collective memory we all hold. Also the memory of our lineage, of our ancestors.

Natural Law is actually memory. We expect Natural Law to happen, and it does. Wood floats; a stone sinks. We expect it, from our past experience and from the collective mind. Everybody agrees on it, remembers it. You might say everything here is made of memory.

The great sages are able to live in full consciousness, making unusual choices, rather than depending on memory to dictate what will happen this moment. For instance, a certain rabbi could place a wick on water, light it on fire, and it would burn. He brought his consciousness to it, so it was outside of Natural Law.

The dreaming state with which we are all familiar, is a place where anything may happen. This is the astral realm, where images make a big splash. It's impressionistic, like an impressionistic painting. It's colorful. As soon as you think of something, there it is. It pops up. But you can't set it on the table and expect it to be there later. You can't build on it.

The sages tell us that in the astral realm we are still learning. Our desire is to be ever closer to God. But the astral is not a place where we can put form and limitation to use the way we can here in the waking state.

The state of deep sleep is something the brain can't even report to us about. The brain is accustomed to measuring changes and remembering them. But in deep sleep there are no changes to record. The brain has nothing to remember.

However, if you maintained awareness during deep sleep, you would be fully enveloped in light, filled with the universal Om sound or a humming. Your feeling-vibration would be one of bliss. These three things – light, Om, and bliss – are the basic materials that go into all form and become the starlight, the birdsong, and all the many details of our waking world.

So the brain is able to focus on any of these three states – waking, dreaming, or deep sleep. But the brain is not consciousness. The brain is limitation. The brain organizes and helps give form. The brain is a tool for you. The brain is not you.

Your consciousness is much larger than your brain. Your consciousness watches as you go into meditation, where you may dip into dreaming or sleeping, even though you're awake. Even if you get only a small taste of this in meditation, it helps with your alignment. It helps you understand that your consciousness, your being, your soul is who you really are. It's much larger than your body, so to speak. It is living in your body but also in other domains beyond your waking state.

On the spiritual path, especially with meditation, it is possible to expand your awareness to witness the dream state while you are awake. This may happen with lucid dreaming, for instance, or with creative inspiration, when you are extremely relaxed and receptive. The astral plane and the physical plane bridge together briefly.

An advanced meditator may slip into the sleep state and witness all three states at once.

The teachers in India tell us that alignment of all three states simultaneously is Samadhi. The yogi in Samadhi is awake and dreaming and in deep sleep, all at the same time. Some yogis have been measured with their brains emitting beta waves, theta, delta waves, all at once.

We don't need to put big expectations on our meditation practice. We are already so familiar with these three states of being. Sometimes they waft in, even a little bit when we meditate. Even that much increases our awareness.

We enjoy collecting knowledge and building upon what we know, what we understand, in this waking world. Yet there comes a point, especially now in this era, when knowledge keeps expanding in every direction. There's no end to it. We can't encompass it. And we discover that knowledge does not bring us happiness.

At this point we feel a shift in ourselves. Knowledge becomes not such a priority anymore. We've read all the books we can hold. What we really want is bliss.

The best we can do is to cultivate lightheartedness. Try to be in a calm place no matter what arises. Accept what is, as it is. We say "Gam zu l' tovah," Everything is for the good. The more we practice this, the more things do turn out well.

The best practice is to let go right in the middle of your tension. On the brink of heightened stress, if you can release it and get calm, then you'll know you're doing well.

Be light and easy. When you feel the same whether you're waiting for a bus or lying down in your bed at the end of a long day, then you're aligned.

62 Bottles in Bottles of Awareness/ Levels of Soul/ Time

If we had a goal, it would be to bring the unconscious to light, bring it to consciousness. The reason Shabbos and all Jewish holidays begin at nightfall is because we are bringing light into our darkness. Bringing more awareness.

When God said, "Let there be light," it meant "Let there be consciousness."

Question: If our progress in this life depends on becoming aware of our unconscious limitations, is this also true of the beings in other realms?

Yes, Isaac replied. In all worlds, all realms, the challenge is to become more and more conscious. Imagine three bottles of increasing size, and they are one inside the other, each with its own cork. Each contains seawater as well as its smaller bottle.

The smallest bottle is our physical existence. When we finish this existence, and the small bottle breaks, we are released into a larger space. We have an experience of expansion into more seawater. It feels liberating. We gain a wider perspective in the astral plane. Yet eventually we find we are limited by the next larger bottle.

All beings want to and need to increase awareness, in order to go beyond all the bottles. By the time we break all the bottles, we re-join the Unity of the Ocean. We melt into It, and we're overjoyed to do so.

Watch and listen to your dreams. Dreams are often the best tool to uncover the unconscious. You might like to jot down a few descriptive words the moment you awaken, to strengthen your remembrance.

Question: Please explain more about the levels of the soul, of increasing consciousness. Are they like the bottles?

Yes, the levels of the soul are the Nefesh, the Ruach, the Neshama, the Chaya, and finally the Yehidah. Only the Yehidah is complete Union.

Among the many names for God, Elokim is the One who forms all things in the world of duality. This is a subject-object world, where the subject is your inner witness, looking at the objects.

Havayah is the name of God that means Unity, and God alone.

Question: It seems like all the holy books, from whatever tradition, are meant to just teach us how to live in duality.

Yes, but more than that. They bring in more spiritual teaching than just duality. We live in a time now where all religions are facing each other. They used to stay in their own isolated places, but now they're all crowded together in the living room, so to speak. Now they're learning tolerance of each other. And we will come together. We will be able to understand each other and remain different. Each culture is unique and will be valued as such.

Comment: The more I live this life, the more it feels like no matter what is happening, I'm not doing it. God is doing it. I'm nobody. But God is pouring through. So it's okay. I'm just splashing, and that's what I'm meant to do.

Question: How is time here different than in other realms?
We tend to speak about the past, present, and future. When we consider our sense of "now" – it feels like it lasts about a second. Now it's gone already. Now it's the next moment.

Our teachers tell us that in the astral realm, "now" is about ten years of our time. So those in the astral simply have a broader view of what's happening here. They may see our future.

Really there's no such thing as time. Time is different widths of perspective.

"Another way to understand this," Isaac said, folding his hands in front of his face, "is to look through a small gap between your hands." He peered through the slit between his hands. "Now I focus on the past, and I see only Shelly. I shift my focus to the present, and I see Donna. Looking to the future, I see Molly. But if I make this gap in my hands wider, I see both past and present, Shelly and Donna, at the same time. Or wider - I see all three - past, present, future."

It's really a case of perspective. Sages gain a wider perspective and more awareness of what-is. The elevator in their metaphorical building works well. Remember how we've said you can see much more, the higher you go in the building. Sages can hold more in their view.

Astral beings simply see a larger scope of "time." In fact our biggest shock of dying can be this sudden widening view, when our "now" enlarges.

Comment: That perspective can keep changing, I think, even with the metaphorical building. At least I find myself looping around, up and down in the building, with expanding and shrinking viewpoints, depending on what's happening.

Yes, Isaac agreed, it certainly is like that. We constantly make adjustments and cope with whatever comes up in our lives.

Question: I want to ask about identity, because our identity seems to go along with those breaking bottles. We may feel or remember that we have lived certain lives, and we have been particular people. Yet when we reach that last bottle and then release into the Ocean, do we discover we were all of it, not limited to any identity? We really were just energy going into different beings, going into everything, all along?

Yes, and in that sense there is no reincarnation, said Isaac. Imagine you had five dreams in one night. Each dream was very real to you. First you were in London, and you had a particular job and family. Then you were in China, doing something else. Then you were in Africa or wherever. Each dream felt like it was so real when you were in it. You could see these as five different lives, because you were completely absorbed in each of them. But the true you is the watcher, the dreamer. Everything happens to these dream people. They may be all tossed around, challenged and changed in any number of ways. But the dreamer does not change.

63 Find God's Delight Inside/ Stand in Gratitude

After wandering a long time in the desert, the people asked if the Promised Land was really worth it, so they sent twelve spies ahead to scope it out.

The spies returned with huge grapes the size of melons. Yet they said the people there were giants, difficult to conquer, and the harsh land consumed its people.

However two of the scouts, Joshua and Caleb, said it was a good idea to go ahead. They said, "If we find God's delight in us, then He will bring us into this land and give it to us – a land that oozes milk and honey."

While ten of twelve saw only obstacles and difficulty, two could see the potential for happiness and ease, if we find God's delight inside us. God will bring us and give it to us. There are no obstacles, no need to conquer.

Can we find God's delight inside ourselves?

It's all about the perspective you take. Always and always, five out of six people see difficulty, while one sees delight. The ten spies were looking at outside appearances, as most people still do today.

Only two knew the truth, the open secret, that you can begin from the inside and go outward. Your inside creates the outside.

This same idea is reflected in our weekly rest and delight on Shabbos. Six days are full of work and obstacles, the "outside" life, while the seventh is to settle into gratitude and happiness, the "inside" life.

Our outside life is not easy. We all face limitations. We all want to fulfill our desires. This is life.

Only God is complete and lacks nothing. Every other being in the universe, right up to the highest angel, is lacking in some way. Every being wants to fill what's lacking in themselves. Every being keeps moving toward completion. That's how the motivation toward growth occurs. The contrast of desire and fear keeps it all rolling.

Now if you're God, complete in Yourself, eternally blissful, why would You create these worlds? We can't really answer that. But we can see how desire and fear motivate us, and how our limitations are part of the whole scheme, to keep it all going.

Our limitations give us our unique abilities.

It's like the way electricity goes into different appliances in the home. One appliance is designed to keep things cold, another to heat up and cook. All of them rely on their source, electricity. In a sense it is all electricity. But what distinguishes one thing from another is its limitations, the way it is designed, what parts it has, what parts it doesn't have. Each thing is important to the household because of its particular qualities.

So, too, we each contribute value according to our qualities. Yes, we have limitations, but that's part of the plan. We don't need to get a headache over it. We don't dwell too much on the parts we don't have. We don't drag ourselves down the road of complaints.

Ten of those scouts to the Promised Land brought back complaints and pessimism. Only two offered optimism. They knew it was all possible, if we find God's delight in us.

How we can "find God's delight" inside us? We turn our attention to satisfaction and completeness. We give thanks for what's already here. We appreciate the very role we play, the very qualities we do have, and the abundance of our life as it is. We let go of the "outside" view and return to the "inside," just as we do on Shabbos. We move to a tone of appreciation and gratitude. We lighten up. This is God's delight in us.

Gratitude is the way. It is the whole way.

It's not about making lists of what to be grateful for. It's about learning to stand in gratitude.

When we descend into our personal swamp, whatever it is, we recognize it. We say, "Oh yes, I've been here before, I know this place, where I feel lost and lacking."

This is the time you need to find anything, by hook or by crook, anything for which you feel grateful. One lighter thought, one note of gratitude, leads to the next. Eventually you have moved yourself, shifted yourself enough to "find God's delight inside."

64 Tainted Grain/ Tricky Ego/ Humility is Contentment

Isaac recounted a story Rabbi Nachman used to tell about a kingdom long ago.

The king and his minister (star gazer) realized that the next year's supply of grain was tainted, poisoned. Not enough to kill people, but enough to make them go crazy. All would have to eat this grain to survive the year. They had nothing else to eat. The minister suggested that he and the king could find some good grain for themselves. But the king pointed out that if they acted sane when all about them were insane, then the people would see the two of them as crazy. The king said we'll have to eat from the same grain. But we'll put an X on each other's foreheads, so at least in the midst of our craziness, when we see the mark on each other, we will remember that we are crazy.

Today here we are, just barely aware that we are crazy in this land. It's a blessing to remember that we are crazy.

At our deepest level, we continue to maintain our ego. To do that, we choose enemies, whether we are aware of them or not. The ego needs an enemy to push up against and define itself. The ego needs to say, "I am not that, I don't do what that person does," as a way to show itself who and what it is. To define itself and give life to itself. The ego makes boundaries for itself. The thicker these boundaries are, the less awareness we have.

But the soul is like water. The soul wants to expand without boundaries. Pour water on a table top, it flows everywhere. That's the soul. Pour water into a glass, and it is contained. It takes on form. Pour the soul into a body, it takes on this form.

Now when my water touches your water, what happens? It melds together. Water has no resistance. It wants to expand, that's all. Water meets water, soul meets soul, and there is no ego confronting ego here.

Our ego is tricky, though. Our ego defenses are built upon deeper defenses. The defense can be convoluted. Maybe we give charity while telling ourselves how grand and important we are for giving that. We may jump up in righteousness to defend a good cause, but in so doing, our ego is yelling about how right and good we are. In other words, the ego uses these "good actions" to pump itself up.

Our teachers say humility is the essential quality we need.

Humility isn't about bowing down to others or negating yourself.

Rather, you humbly play your role, in service to the One. When you're humble, you are happy with yourself just as you are. Warts and all. You are so joyful and content, nothing ruffles you. That's why you are immune to praise or blame. Everybody else's opinion simply doesn't matter, because you are secure.

Humility means contentment. Humility is Presence. Presence and contentment.

The rabbis of the yeshiva in Russia years ago would send their students to the hardware store to ask for a bag of apples. Not to make them suffer, but to give their ego a challenge, to be lambasted by the shopkeeper. They learned to relax into insults without defending their ego.

Comment: The self-critical ego makes an enemy of itself.
Yes, we certainly deal with self-criticism. It can be very subtle, even when we have trained our ego to say mostly nice things to us.

Sometimes people cannot own their positive characteristics, because they have such a low opinion of themselves. You tell them, "You have this beautiful quality," but they pass it off, they don't believe it. They are so hungry for love but they have a long-standing pattern of denying love for themselves even when it is offered. Or maybe they have come far enough to accept the compliment in a seemingly graceful way, yet they shove it off to the side, into their secret trash can. They simply can't receive it.

Question: Where can we find peace?
The way is not a straight ascent, as a child would expect. Instead it goes up and down unpredictably. You may reach a high plateau and think you have really succeeded in making progress with your ego. But then suddenly you drop again. All of this is to be expected. No matter who we are, our buttons can get hit, and we shift into "story-land" again, where the ego tells monumental stories.

65 Livelihood/ God is Abundant

The simplest way to receive livelihood is straight from God.

King David said, "God, feed us with Will." This shows an understanding that all we experience, every bit of it, arises from God and is created every moment. Even your livelihood comes from God, not from your own efforts.

The world is our mirror. The world isn't so much external as it is internal. Every person is thus living in their own world, allowing or disallowing whatever comes to them.

God is abundant toward you at all times. But when your perception is shut down, when your view becomes narrow and critical of things, God seems restrictive. You have in fact restricted yourself inside, so that's what shows up on your outside, in your circumstances.

Poverty may be related to flawed perception of the abundance you do have.

Illness is related to flawed perception of your abundant health.

David spoke about how tzaddikim, saints, blossom like palm trees. When you understand fully, your crown blossoms like the top of a palm tree. Then you know everything you receive comes directly from God and is being created right now.

So relax into this, right at this moment. Realize that all the objects of your desires, whether material or non-material, are already within you. Already abundant.
Already given to you by God.
Already there.
Do you see how this perspective releases the striving? You don't have to want anything. It's already there for you.

You'll notice it's not the rich man who walks down the street, muttering an affirmation, "I'm rich, I'm rich." No, that's for those who feel lacking. The rich man already knows he has plenty of money and takes it in stride. You already are the rich man. You need only to open your awareness, your contentment.
When you can be in a state of contentment, fully aware that everything is from God, and there's nothing more to want, then your yearning has no function. It falls away. Everything is already within you. Everything is already yours. You're not missing anything.

66 White Light, All Vibrations, Prism to Colors/ Swami Rama

Unity coming into Duality is like white light going through a prism. White light contains all colors. With a prism it separates into all the colors of the rainbow. Red, orange, yellow, green, blue, indigo, violet. These are different vibrations.

White light is all vibrations. Every color has a distinct vibration, different from the other colors.

Some colors go together and are complimentary towards each other. Some don't. This is the way of musical notes, as well. They vibrate differently. When you play two notes together, they may be harmonious or dissonant.

If we see ourselves as a color or a note, it's only natural that we would enjoy those who are harmonious with us, and reject those who aren't. It's difficult to enjoy what is not "you" or what is not in harmony with you.

Also, in this world of separateness, the more something is defined as a particular vibration, then it cannot be another vibration. It feels what is missing. If it is identified as one color, it can't be another color.

So the yearning, the desire to possess what is "not you" -- is natural to this rainbow world. For instance, on the topic of money – say you are in the red, and you want green. As long as you stay with the mindset of the rainbow world, you are separate from your desire. But if you go to a mindset of completion, go to the white light world which contains everything, then you know you are both red and green, you are all the colors together. There is no "want" in the white light world. You have embraced all vibrations, and there is no lack. You have everything. Desire has dissolved.

Question: So we don't have to reject our desires, as so many ascetics have suggested. If we reach the broad view of things, desire just leaves?

Yes, those ascetic teachers were moving in the right direction, but they didn't have the whole picture. Desire lives on the rainbow side of the prism, but on the white light side it simply dissolves.

This isn't to say that the journey to the white light is easy. It's not easy to embrace things that are dissonant to you. Dissonance sounds bad, looks bad. Yet if we can recognize that we are actually made of all vibrations, not just the narrow vibration we thought we were – then we can be on the white light side and experience that contentment. The white light is who we really are. It's always available to us.

Comment: It reminds me of trying to explain the concept of air to a child. You can't see it, but it surrounds us, and it's vital to us. I also find it fascinating that in order to have creation, you have to have restriction. You have to withhold other vibrations in order to show a distinctive color vibration.

Yes, said Isaac, creation is an aspect of Gevurah, which is constriction.

When we meditate deeply, we can reach that white light, which feels like a humming of all things. At the same time, it is nothing distinctive. Everything loses distinction. No borders or boundaries. It's just a hum. Blissful hum, like the bliss of deep sleep.

If you had awareness of your deep sleep, you would know there is nothing defined there, no aspect to record and bring back with you. It is simply all light. So it seems to be nothing. Like air. Yet it restores us.

The great yogis are able to experience their waking state, dreaming state, and deep sleep simultaneously. When a person is able to do that, they are so close to the Source of all things. It's like you're at a window where the sunlight is pouring through. You can bask in the warm sun, but there's still a barrier of glass between you and the sun. You are nearly melted into Unity, yet still here in Duality.

This is when a yogi can instantly manifest things, straight from God, because they have access to the higher levels. They bypass Natural law. They know everything arises from God each moment. Anything is possible to them, and so it is.

Swami Rama tells about how he was sitting under a tree next to a river for months, and after awhile nobody brought him any food. They came to visit, but they brought no food.

He said, "Okay God, if You want me to eat, You'll provide. And if You don't want me to eat, that's fine, I don't mind dying." He was surrendered to the Will. He became quite weak.

One day a hand rose out of the river, bearing a bowl for him. This was a miraculous bowl that would constantly fill with food. He would eat from it, and it would refill itself.

People started coming from miles around to see this bowl. They weren't so interested in hearing his teachings. They just wanted to see the bowl fill up.

Swami Rama asked his teacher what to do about this. The teacher said to throw the bowl back into the river. The miracle had served its purpose and was of no use any more. So he returned it to the river.

Apart from deep meditation, there are other ways to be in the white light state. When you do only what is in front of you right this moment, it's a way of connecting to white light. You're fully Present. You're in the flow.

Think of a mother with a bunch of kids, and they're jumping around, messing things up. It's all she can do to relax and not yell at them, much less clean up anything yet. She is forced to let go of whatever doesn't absolutely have to be done right now. She handles only what arises in the moment that must be done.

This is when we live in the "Gam zu l'tovah" state of mind. We remind ourselves, "This too is for the good."

67 Rosh Hashanah – New Year

God is all of this, and beyond. Our minds and the equipment we have for living in this dimension are limited, such that we cannot fully fathom God. We cannot speak of God, really. We cannot possibly define or encapsulate the All. It extends for so many worlds beyond ours. We have barely a glimpse of It.

Before the New Year begins, the Old Year must end. We must go to the state of nothingness, releasing the old year. We must be empty.

Imagine standing in a pool of pure Being. Stillness. This pool's surface is as glassy as a mirror. The sun is perfectly reflected in it. Only One sun.

If we start some waves in this pool, we will see the reflections of many suns. Diversity. Duality.

You and I are these waves, these reflections. Our world is made up of a multitude of these reflections. So much variety.

All worlds are made of these waves and reflections of the One. Every world carries its own band of frequencies.

In this world of action and doing, Assiyah, we have a particular band of frequencies unique to our world. We are born with the proper equipment to deal in these frequencies. Here we have everything from vengeful anger to peace. And everything in-between.

Even scientists tell us that we are made up of waves. Brain waves. Heart waves. Every cell and molecule, down to the smallest part, is actually waves.

Everything in our world can be recognized by its own frequency. Each thing vibrates differently than anything else. We know this.

As we emerge into the next world, we find it is composed of frequencies that feel new and different to us, yet we already have the equipment to sense those frequencies. In the astral world of Yetzirah, space falls away. In the world of doing, when we travel from New York to London, we have to cover ground in some way, either by plane or by ship. But in the astral plane, we can be there immediately, just by thinking it. And there we go, in a flash, as we move from class to class. We keep learning.

In the third world of Beriah, time falls away. We have access to all time in the Now of Beriah. All the past and future is available.

Think how it is, if we are all in a swimming pool together: one person might be on a raft with a drink in his hand, somebody else swimming, maybe another sitting on a watery step meditating in the sunshine. Here comes somebody else, suddenly splashing up waves. So the guy on the raft spills his drink. Everybody is affected in some way. Even if it was just a small wave, the raft will bob.

We live in a shared pool. Everything we do has an effect far beyond what we realize. We're interconnected. We affect each other.

Rosh Hashanah is like a seed day for the whole year. The way a seed contains the future plant. So what you do today influences this year, the sages would say.

I wish you blessings this year, that you should have happiness in your family and relationships, good health and a good prosperous livelihood, sweetness in all aspects of your life.

This year may you have a good governor of the mouth. Sometimes holding back our words is better than spilling words we will regret. When we say something insensitive, we can ask for and receive forgiveness. But in the long run, people don't forget what was said. It happened and you can't fully erase it.

It's best to develop a good governor of the mouth.

The way to govern the mouth on the face is to govern the mouth in the mind. This can be done only when there is a Witness watching what it says.

And certainly the way to strengthen your inner Witness is to engage in meditation. This naturally leads to good self-observation and clarity.

Now if you like, you can reset yourself, with your eyes closed. Go to nothing. Empty out the old year. Make space for the new year to come in.

68 Light in All Things/ World Made of Wisdom/ Atzilut

There is a light, an energy, that permeates all worlds and gives rise to everything that exists in all worlds. We could say that all worlds are composed of it.

This energy is Chochmah, wisdom. In the eastern tradition it is known as Prana. It's the energy that fuels everything.

We know this because the Torah tells us, "God, you have made the world with wisdom," meaning wisdom is like the building blocks for the world. Everything emanates from wisdom.

The highest world Atzilut is a place of archetypes. Ideas are formed in Atzilut. We cannot recognize Atzilut with our human minds, because it is before thought. The closest we might come is to call it the world of intuition. Even "intuition" doesn't fully convey what it is. Manifestation begins in this place, where the formless begins to take form.

The great name of God, if we look at the letters, also teaches us how the world comes into being. Yod-Hey-Vav-Hey. The first letter, the Yod, which looks like a little comma, has a tiny spike at the top, and this is the crown. The top of the sefirot, our divine connection at the crown of our head. Yod represents Atzilut.

Below Atzilut the idea or intuition passes through the level of Thought, and gains more form. The level of Thought corresponds to the second letter in the name of God, which is Hey. Then this particular idea comes into the layer of Emotion - the letter Vav. Finally this idea manifests in the Physical realm - the second letter Hey.

Visualize an apple. See its color and its form in detail. Notice we don't all visualize at the same rate. Your apple may be hazy, like the screen image on an old television with rabbit ears, where the reception comes and goes. That's okay. Visualize to whatever degree you are able.

The eyes correlate to Chochmah and Yod, the first letter in the great name of God, because visualization is the first step in creation. Just as Atzilut is the first step in creation. So the more fully you can visualize something, the more easily it becomes real.

We think that when we have negative daydreams, when we imagine getting revenge or such like that, we think it has no repercussions in the world. But as our teachers have said, all visualizations rise to the highest levels, to Atzilut, and eventually they do take on form. They emanate gradually back into this world.

Many spiritual traditions would ask students to first visualize something, like our apple, and bring it into sharper and sharper focus, all the details of it. Does your apple have streaks? What shape is the stem? Is it symmetrical? Does it have any spots or bruises?

Now bring in another of your senses. Feel the weight of the apple in your hand. If you scratch it, you can smell the apple. The more senses you bring in fully, the more real this apple-image becomes, until there is very little difference between the image and reality.

Some would say we're still dealing with imagination here, but if we were able to do this fully, we would be holding a real apple in our hands. This is how sages can manifest objects out of thin air. They do so only to reveal God's presence, or to teach in some way.

Others may learn to do this, but they misuse it, because they haven't mastered their ego.

As we go into meditation today, if you wish, you can focus on light and energy, the Chochmah or Prana flowing through your body. Focus on it and feel it.

Remember, as we have said before, when your mind wanders and you bring it back, this is like strength training. You keep lifting the same weight.

If you lift a hundred pounds one time, will it make you strong? No. It is the repetition of lifting the same weight many times that makes you stronger.

In the same way, repeating the action of redirecting your focus will make your meditation stronger. It is cumulative. The more often you practice, the easier it will become to find your focus.

69 Sukkot/ Simcha Joy/ Amalek, Doubt and Trust

Our teachers say that simcha - joy - is really not of this world. Simcha comes from beyond this world. It comes through certain places, people, and times. Sukkot is such a time, when joy arrives from beyond this world. It is our most joyful holiday. Children especially have a fun time at Sukkot, because living in the sukkah shelter is like camping. Kids feel a freedom here. Freedom is joy.

Some sages would say that to be forced to work for a living is like a curse. The world is so abundant, everything could be provided. In our time, things are different, and we are accustomed to work in order to feed ourselves.

Simcha (joy) and freedom go hand in hand. We might define our joy by saying my joy is money, I need enough money. Or my joy is in my relationships. Or I love to travel. But on Sukkot we're speaking about a deeper joy.

The Shekhinah, divine presence, rests on the sukkah. In fact it is written that the roof of the sukkah can only be so high. This is because the roof is a portal of joy, and if it's too high above our heads, we may not be able to feel it. Of course this flow of joy is the reason the roof needs to be hole-y, full of holes, allowing sunshine and rain to pour in. We don't stop things from flowing in, because all things are blessings.

Sukkot is a special time for anybody on a spiritual path, because the divine flow of this season brings your next knowledge to you. This knowledge is still outside your experience. You have no words for it yet. But it's almost yours. It arrives with the most subtle hints. The sages say this knowledge is like an aura around your head, just on the verge of coming in. Or you could see it as if you were climbing stairs, and this is your next step.

May there be blessings of joy and new beginnings for all of us.

It's amazing how God's hand is in everything. In this season it is perhaps more visible than usual. We never know how things come into play, but often we see that we are guided, even in the little things. It helps if we are listening. We take whatever hint arises.

It's important to trust that the next hint is indeed coming.

Amalek is another word for doubt. It was Amalek who chased the Israelites through the desert for forty years. No matter where they went, he hounded them relentlessly. Doubt.

So our doubt chases us and makes it difficult for us to receive our joy and freedom.

Whatever it is in your own life that pursues you with doubt, take a look at it.

This is the time to release doubt.

Trust in the divine flow coming to you. To you, personally, in whatever shape or form is appropriate for you. God is answering.

This will build your trust in God.

You hear about these biblical people who lived a few hundred years? I always thought that wasn't literally true, but it actually was true. They did live that long. How could that be possible? Because their trust was so sure. They had no doubt they were meant to keep going.

Whenever Moses raised his hands in prayer, Amalek would stop chasing. When we have that divine connection of prayer, that stance of asking for divine help, doubt dissipates.

But when Moses grew tired and his hands fell to his sides, that position is "I'm alone and doing it all myself." Then doubt closes in. Amalek draws closer.

It's written that Amalek captured all the stragglers who couldn't keep up, or who left the group. They had slipped out of the sacred cloud that always rested on the community.

Your chosen community supports you and increases your trust. This is one of the strengths of community. Interdependence, the give and take, the net of friendship, brings us stability, resilience, and great blessing.

70 Lech Lecha, Release/ The Horizontal and The Vertical

The Torah Portion "Lech Lecha" (Genesis 12:1-17:27) portrays the moment when God tells Abram to go, to leave his homeland. What would it be like to release your family, your country, your very identity? What would that look like?

It would be like, you're in your car on your way to a new job interview, something important, and you make a wrong turn and get lost. You feel panic rising in you. You know the more you panic, the more messed up and lost you will get, you are getting. But if you can release, if you can pretend it's not so important, if you can step back and hold your identity lightly, then you allow clarity to come in. Don't take it seriously, and it lightens up. A moment ago you were a vital professional applicant, but now you're just a person on an unknown street. Breathing, rolling along. Your inner peace allows divine help to come.

Remember the horizontal and the vertical. The horizontal life is the practical way we live our life, our jobs, our families. The horizontal is founded on the past. Because of our past, we think we know pretty much what our future will be. We react to events according to what we know about them from our past. It worked this way last time, therefore I predict the same, and all my expectations are reinforced.

Past memories perpetuate our fears and desires. We predict more of the same.

Many of us may live our whole lives in the horizontal, not touching the vertical very often. We can manage the horizontal. But the more we remain in the horizontal without visits to the vertical, the more dry life becomes.

The vertical is the Present, without judgment. No fear, no desire. It just is. The vertical shows us that everything here, despite appearances, IS the Divine Will coming into being this moment, into the physical. When we are in the vertical, we can see and accept this, without any opinions.

Opinion belongs in the horizontal. Opinion requires a past to make it work.

In the vertical there is no past. Everything simply is, and we take it as it is. No opinions about it.

In our meditation thoughts will always arise. They come to me, they come to you. We're not going to stop them, really. But the key, if you remember nothing else, the key is an attitude of disinterest in those thoughts.

How do you handle traffic noise? Either it bothers me and I can't stand it, or I allow it to be there. After awhile I hardly notice it. Think of your chattering thoughts as traffic noise. Just allow all to be as it is.

Thought and emotion create the horizontal world. Thought often arises first, and we choose to react to it. Some don't realize they have a choice - they react automatically. But if we could slow down the process, we would see that a thought arises, we choose to react, we hook into it with our emotion, and now it's real. If we weren't hooked into it with emotion, then it wouldn't matter to us. It wouldn't affect us. It wouldn't be "real" to us. Our emotion about it makes it big, important, defines it to us.

When you form opinions and emotions, when you have words about it, you define it. You give it a solid shape. You encapsulate it. You pigeonhole it and put it where it belongs in your world.

It's not like we can stay in the vertical all the time, either. You're not going to be frozen in Samadhi and not function in ordinary life. When you bring more of the vertical into your life, your life will not be much different. You'll most likely have your same job, your family, everything. But you'll be seeing it all differently.

God doesn't come to earth in an otherworldly way, with bright lights and all that.

God enters this world and becomes form. When you're connected to the vertical, you see the way the physical world represents God, the way it is God.

The point is, God is invisible in this world. Invisible and omnipresent. But God enters through form, because this world is form.

How do you know you are connecting with the vertical more than you used to? It happens when you're under some stress, some difficulty, and you notice you don't scream as loud as you used to. You're calmer. You face things more easily. You have some space, some release. Lech Lecha.

We're talking about a blended world, where you are in both horizontal and vertical. You need both here.

While the horizontal has its ups and downs, almost like a rollercoaster, a long wavy line, the vertical is like a hum all the time, a straight line running right through the center of the wavy line. The vertical connection is a hum - "Ommm" in the background.

The Taoists always look for harmony in their world, wherever they are.

No matter what is happening, see harmony in it.

Don't look for spiritual phenomena. I might share stories about phenomena, and certainly I have been blessed to see much of that, and it's all true. But if you get attached to phenomena, you get off-track. It doesn't lead to God. That's not its purpose. Its purpose is to loosen you up from your dry assumptions, your old horizontal certainties.

If your meditations grow to be amazing and wonderful, and you start telling yourself, "Isaac's having a good time," what have you done? You took the wordless, opinion-less vertical, and you made it horizontal. You defined and pigeonholed your experience, and you probably moved your ego up a few notches. All you did was to make a more exotic horizontal.

71 Stay Out of the Story/ Gaze at God/ Av Harachaman

As we go into meditation, remember to watch your thoughts.

There you are, settling in, and you see yourself in conversation with someone you dislike. Suddenly the thought comes in: "I wish you'd die."

We're not here to judge any thought, but to acknowledge that everybody has unbidden thoughts, from the beginning meditator to the tzaddik. You won't ever get rid of thoughts. The approach is to observe them and not go with them.

This isn't like swatting flies. If you fight or resist thoughts, you are entering into a relationship with them. That's not what you want. Rather, you want to watch them arise and depart, with or without any emotion attached to them. Both thought and emotion may arise and flow through, without you attaching yourself.

Thoughts are invitations to veer out of your meditation. Do you give your consent to that thought? Do you jump in and participate with it, or not? At what point do you consent to it? From that moment, you begin to create a story and get sidetracked away from your meditation.

See if you can just observe those thoughts, whatever they may be, without consenting to join in the story they want to tell.

Let's begin silent meditation . . .

Question: The Sh'ma prayer makes reference to things men do, such as the wearing of tefillin. How can a woman make that more of her own prayer, if she doesn't do the things men do?

Isaac replied that when we pray, we are all in the feminine mode. We pray with our soul, our Neshama, which is feminine. Every reference to the soul is always feminine. This is because all of creation is receiving from the Source of all. The Source is constantly giving, and we are always receiving.

The deeper meaning of our prayers, even when they make reference to men or masculine things, is really all about receptivity. Some sages spoke about how the very letters of the Torah are conduits to God. Just looking upon the letters can bring in the divine presence. You can place the name of God in front of you and gaze upon it, meditate upon it.

In our meditation, we are all working toward a pure heart, like our song tells us, "Lev Tahor." Create in me a pure heart.

God's blessings are always flowing, but we need to make a cup to hold the blessings. This is what we do in meditation. We empty our thoughts so we become like a cup. If we don't build a space to hold the blessings, we may not realize they're even flowing. But they always are.

God is constantly gazing at us, and sometimes we can gaze back. It's like two lovers who look into each other's eyes.

They don't have to say anything. Their eyes, their connection, says it all. In just this way, God looks at us, all the time.

The amazing thing is when we can engage in that gaze and at the same time deal with the functional details of our lives. To experience absorption and detail at the same time. Vertical and horizontal. You'd think that would be impossible, but it's natural, because God fills the world every moment.

Comment: It's like -- I drive my kids across town a lot, and I'm all over the freeway. When I feel Connected, traffic parts for me, the cars just leave the perfect gaps, and I slip around so easily and safely. But when I'm not Connected, then the traffic is crazy, and I can't get to the exit, and driving becomes almost dangerous.

That's a perfect example, said Isaac.

The challenge of settling the thoughts is so difficult, sometimes we might want to begin again to learn to meditate. Try to watch exactly what happens inside you at the moment when you consent to the thought. Find the moment just before you begin to create the story around the thought or emotion. Find that spot, see it, live in it. Feel the type of energy in it.

My inner image of this moment is a mouse eating the cheese. The mouse is the ego. The cheese is the thought or story. My mouse wants that cheese. But I can relax and say no, not this time.

Question: How can we stay in constant meditation?

We can take any short phrase or mantra or prayer from any tradition, but the key is to make it short. Whatever the phrase is, approach it not as a request but as a point of focus, a habitual connection.

As you say that phrase to yourself, it becomes more and more comfortable. At first it may not be so comfortable to pronounce, but you'll get smoother. You breathe into the phrase, repeating it over and over.

It begins as a personal prayer, a connection that you are initiating, but it evolves over time to the point where that phrase seems to say itself, all around you, and you find yourself in a field of Presence. A whole field of endless Presence may be revealed to you, where everything is coherently interacting with everything else.

There is a practice you may want to try, only if you want to, using the phrase:

"Av ha-ra-kha-man, ra-khaym a-lye." ("Av harachaman rachem alai")

"Merciful (loving) Father, have mercy (love) upon me."

You'll remember the teaching that we have two mouths, one up in our head and one on our face. The first mouth is mental and belongs to the world of thought. The world of Beriah, also known as the causal plane. Things arise in thought before they become physical.

With this prayer, first bow your head and say it in your mind as you breathe in, lifting your head. Tilt your face slightly up to heaven. Then as you breathe out, say the prayer aloud with your mouth and bow your head down again.

Repeat this for a few minutes.

You are voicing the prayer first in the world of Beriah, where your mental mouth has its home. That's where your mental voice is. Then you bring the prayer aloud to the physical world. So this practice is joining the two worlds together.

Isaac said when he has done this practice, all kinds of old pains and shortcomings arise in his mind. Places where he fell short in taking care of relationships, either consciously or unintentionally. This practice can be quite soothing.

He suggests to do this only a short while, 15 minutes or so. You may then sit there and find you have a blank mind.

72 Tiferet, Balance of Strength and Loving-kindness

Avraham (Abraham) is the embodiment of Chesed, loving-kindness. His son Isaac is considered to be the purest Gevurah - strength, discipline, strictness. Isaac's eldest son Esau is too much Gevurah, too powerful. His second son Jacob is Tiferet, which is balance, beauty, the integration of loving-kindness and discipline.

The biblical story of Jacob taking the inheritance seems to tell us power does not inherit. This must speak to our own sense of power or powerlessness.

We locate Tiferet at our heart, the center of our chest. It is balance -- knowing when to use strength and strictness, when to use loving-kindness. But this is not a mental decision. It's a deeper knowing. It's the ability to be appropriate to the moment. It may be using power in service to loving-kindness.

When Tiferet truly arises, it changes our behavior. Our life may look the same, but our approach to it changes.

We can't force our way into Tiferet, or into better behavior. It may look like we can use our mind to convince ourselves that this reaction is better than that one. It's a common approach, to let our mind run our life.

Really when people use their power in efforting with their mind to control behavior, it looks like two hands pressing hard against each other (prayer position). There is tremendous effort, but no movement. You can exhaust yourself, pushing your mind against your behavior. You're going nowhere, but you look "good" (pun of praying hands).

In order to find your way to real Tiferet, remember the analogy of the projector light bulb which shines through the film. The light is always on, always available. The film, which is the mind, limits the amount of light coming through. In the darker or brighter scenes, we see how Mind affects the world.

We live in a vibratory world. Everything is vibration, and in a sense all the world is of the mind. The world is the movie playing in front of us, and our mind sucks us into the story.

The idea is not to force your behavior with your mind, but to go deeper into awareness and begin to understand that the light bulb behind the film gives life to everything.

When Tiferet arises or opens, behavior changes naturally. Virtues arise without effort. You know about the light behind the film.

In our meditation, that light bulb is a place of solidness. It's hard to describe in words. It's quiet and solid and always present, underneath everything.

Like the Torah conveys: "I am God, I do not change."

For some people that steadiness, where nothing seems to happen, is a place of boredom. They say, "Meditation? Sit there and do nothing?" Boredom is the worst thing ever, for them. In fact when they have nothing to do, they may invent drama, trouble in their lives, just to avoid boredom. Boredom is deadly for them.

Don't approach this and say mentally, "Oh yeah, I can meditate, even though my thoughts are running." You need to really go there and experience that place of no words, no mind. Experience that solidity. When you find comfort in that empty solid place, it means you can handle your own death.

When the mind approaches death, it has one of two reactions. Either it's annihilation or it's "I'm about to lose all I've gained."

But if you have found the comfort of the empty solid place, you've gone beyond the mind, and you feel okay to go into the greater awareness beyond death.

You know you're not really here. Think about that. You're not really here at all. You're just projecting parts of yourself here. You are just a pair of eyes looking out at the world. Notice how you don't even see your own face while you participate in the world.

You are a character created to go out from the Light and then spend all your time seeking It again.

In this vibratory mind-driven world, you are living through the character of your mind. Many just live it out, unaware.

But when you go deeper, you will sense the vibration of it. The Eastern traditions call it "Om" -- the vibratory sound that can always be heard.

Can you bring a deeper awareness into your life? Can you take a larger perspective and say, "This too is for the good" - "Gam zu l' tovah?"

On the inside you're saying, "There is nothing wrong."

On the outside you're saying, "What's next?" And you're okay with whatever comes.

Question: Is Daas (a.k.a. Da'at) part of all this?

Daas is the pathway of knowledge, which goes up the central column through Tiferet and ends at Keter, the crown. Keter reveals that whatever we thought "we" were doing in this life, all of it was the Divine Will. Who you are changes completely when you reach Keter. The kabbalists have little to say about Keter. There are no words at Keter.

This isn't to say we're off the hook for our actions in the world. Of course we feel responsible for any pain we've brought to anyone, intentionally or unintentionally. We all have regrets for angry words we've spoken. I have regrets too, like anybody.

Our teachers tell us our regret for past behavior is also a way of ascension.

Teshuva - returning, reconciling - existed before the world was made. The sages say that teshuva, and repairing mistakes, is needed and blessed.

When you consider regrets, or making teshuva, don't sink into sorrow about your past behavior. It's a fine line, looking at regrets. Don't say "I failed." Don't call your life a failure. It's not.

Question: How can we deal with regrets?
Pray. A lot. "God, create in me a pure heart." (Psalm 51.)

73 Connection/ Light Above Clouds/ Return the Gaze

You can find lots of mysticism and mysteries on the spiritual path. You can read many books on all kinds of good practices and try them all. The multitude of books can influence us to take an intellectual stance. The books are good maps, but they're not enough.

No matter how much information we have, what we really need is to find the right vibration of connection with God. The difference between an intellectual understanding and the ability to find the right vibration is like the difference between a mapmaker and one who actually goes to the place. It's easy and comfortable to make a map. Easy to sit around reading and enjoying maps. But to actually go to the sacred place oneself, this is different than looking at maps.

No matter how dark things may feel in our life, remember there is light above the clouds. The sun is always shining.

We tend to see the world below the clouds, where we have important concerns. But in meditation we can get past the clouds to the light. The light fills everything on earth whether we can see it or not. Divine Light hides from us, it's hidden in the world. Yet it's always available. The sages call it "Or ha-Ganus" – the hidden light of creation, above the clouds.

There's a popular understanding that God surrounds you and fills you the way a fish is filled with and surrounded by water. But this metaphor is also missing the mark. Because to us, water is a neutral substance, without any particular meaning.

It would be much more accurate to say we are filled with and surrounded by a warm, loving, alive Presence that cares about each of us personally. It's alive. It's moving. It gives life to us in every moment. It gives life to everything we touch and see, to everybody.

God's attention gives life to us, now, and now, and in the next now. We are here doing this now because of God's attention upon us. If His attention wavered, we might dissolve right now, fading out and in again like the characters on a fuzzy TV screen, the old TV with the rabbit ears antenna.

You don't fade out, though, because God looks upon you continuously.

If God is gazing at you 24/7, you might find time to look back, every now and then. When one of us turns our attention to gaze at God, it's like when two lovers, who have known each other awhile and fully understand each other, look into each other's eyes. Something happens there. The world around them disappears. They are in a different place, together.

So it is when you return the gaze God is giving to you. The sages call it "histaklut" – gazing at God.

This form of prayer, of returning the gaze, is so different than asking for things we want, like "please find a better job for me, help my sick friend."

To "return the gaze," you go to that place of light above the clouds.

When you sit to meditate, to find this vibration of connection, how do you do it? You sit, maybe in a mood of waiting, maybe wondering about your sore legs or your lunch. But you take a moment. Let yourself feel you are being watched right now by God's loving gaze. Become aware of that Divine attention. So you return the gaze.

Feel yourself in a field of light. Try it.

I go to a field of light. I am immersed in it. I am part of it. It's like an ocean. I feel myself as one drop in it. We have the subtle awareness that we are still ourselves, yet we are part of the light, part of the ocean, just on the verge of losing our identity. It's wonderful.

It's simple. Some people tell me it's too simple. It can't be this easy. They want to look further, read more books, find more practices. I say, okay. I'll see you later when you get tired.

There was a Christian monk who wrote about an intense light that appeared while he was praying in his cell. He prayed continuously, as people do, as a way of keeping the attention on God. He had only one candle in his room, yet while he made his usual prayers, a light grew brighter and brighter, too bright for his eyes. He spoke about visions and insights given to him that night.

The next day he went to see a friend on the next mountain. He asked what time it was - midmorning. The monk thought it was still night time. As he'd walked over, the daylight seemed like moonlight, so dim compared to the light he'd seen in his room.

He received this Divine light in the midst of his continuous praying.

It's the prayer, the looking back at God, that brings in the light.

Prayers and mantras are meant to capture your attention back toward God. The knotted fringe of the tzitzit is to help you remember. Judaism carries all kinds of daily reminders like this, things you can see and touch, each of them telling you, "Remember."

Hundreds of years ago there lived a rabbi who had absorbed every teaching from every book, all the practices in depth, far more than anyone else of his era. People asked him, what do you do when you pray?

He replied, "I throw away all those mysteries, and I pray like a child."

Approach as a child approaches a parent who loves them and attends them constantly. The child plays with his toys, but then he sees the most wondrous thing is his parent, who gazes upon him with such love. He leaves his toys to get a hug. This feels so much better than toys.

But then he wants to go back to his toys, just as we do, back to the desires of the world. And that's fine with our divine parent.

It's a balance for us, because we live in both places: underneath the clouds, and above the clouds, in the Light.

74 Walk a Higher Level/ Patriarchs' Attributes/ Larger Self

Question: Is it possible to bring loving-kindness into business transactions?

As we know, oftentimes business is straight business, precision, a fair price for what is offered.

Our teachers tell us every aspect of life is a particular attribute, and each of those attributes contains a subset of all the attributes. So no attribute is purely itself and nothing else. Everything is blended. Many possibilities are open.

At times when the situation calls for it, we let business fall away and treat each other on a purely human level, because both giver and receiver are human. When we are generous in this way, it's not for "the write-off." It's different. It's giving from the heart.

Yes, we can blend loving-kindness with business at times.

Question: I can get into a place of wisdom and peace, but then I forget, and I become so angry. Please give us suggestions on how to not forget, how to remember our place and remember the teachings?

Isaac returned to the metaphor of the multi-leveled building. You visit a higher level, and you like it. You feel comfortable there with a larger more peaceful perspective. But then you fall back to your usual floor, to your accustomed vibration that you have kept in the past. Why can't you stay on the higher floor?

It's like when a toddler is learning to walk. The child's fists hold the parent's forefingers, and the parent leads the toddler. You were led to that higher floor, where your Divine Parent helped you walk. But the Parent lets go, so you can walk by yourself. Perhaps you're almost strong enough to walk on that level. But then, you couldn't manage it, so you fell to your former vibration, your former level.

The first thing is to not berate yourself for having fallen down. Learn that it's okay to fall. In fact it can be a good thing, because after you fall back to your old vibration, those people around you on that lower floor find that you inspire them. You visited the higher place. They look to you, and you become like an elevator to help others visit the place where you went before.

What will strengthen you? The habit of your practices will strengthen you. Don't stop learning. Keep meditating every day, even when you think you know so much that you don't have to bother. Perhaps most days you feel bliss in your meditation, and you look forward to it. But on the days you don't feel like meditating, you should still go to your meditation seat.

Another way to fall down is to presume you know this expanded level "like the back of your hand." Growing complacent is a mistake. Rising to higher levels is a Gift to you. You are brought there and taught to walk. You wouldn't be there unless you were holding onto your Parent's fingers.

As time goes on, by habitually engaging in your practices, you will learn to walk on that higher level yourself. You'll stay there longer and longer.

It's written that Noah walked with God. This means God was leading him by the hands, helping him stay on that level. But Abraham walked before God, which means he was spiritually strong enough to keep himself on a high level.

Sometimes you may be thrown back to one of the lower floors on purpose, for the good of the collective group, who need you to be their elevator up to the next level. In those cases you may ask yourself, why did I fall? You'll find no reason, except that you were needed to help the collective.

The Rabbi of Chernobyl would see people and lift them in this way. After every visit, each session, his clothes were soaking wet with sweat. His assistant rabbi would bring him a fresh set of clothes before each visitor came in. When asked about it, the Rabbi of Chernobyl explained, "First I have to put on their Self, then I put my Self on, then I go back and put on their self." (Higher Self, lower self of each.) Up-down, up-down the elevator. He exerted himself a lot to shift vibrations that much. It was sweating work.

You'll notice a therapist who has personally been through the same difficulty as their client, is more able to guide that client. Another therapist may say the same important suggestions, yet if they have not walked where that client has walked, their words simply don't do enough. They haven't been to the same depths of the elevator as their client.

We on this plane are like the many roots of a plant. When we learn something, we bring that learning up to the higher levels of our soul. We are feeding our larger Self, with everything we do here, just as a root absorbs nutrients and sends them higher.

You may feel like it's too cold and dark down here on earth, and all you see are the other roots. You may not realize what an important job you are doing, supporting your whole plant, helping your larger Self grow with your growth.

The root that you are branches upward into a larger thicker root, and this is the root belonging to your whole family or your soul-mates, your soul group. If you recognize someone as a soul-mate, they may belong to that larger higher root.

The higher you go up this plant, the larger and more beautiful it becomes.

And you are an essential part of it.

Question: We have learned about such a perfect balance between Abraham (Chesed), Isaac (Gevurah), and Jacob (Tiferet). This seems like a complete balance. So what's the rest of the Torah teaching us?

There are more attributes to learn, in order to bring Chesed, Gevurah, and Tiferet into our lives on a practical level. We need these to bring balance into being. The attributes of Hod and Netzach belong to the legs and tell us when to hold back and when to step in. We have a lot to learn from Aaron (Hod), Moses (Netzach), and Joseph (Yesod).

These are people to emulate, but they were real, and they were not perfect. Moses hit the rock when God asked him to speak to the rock. Because of that, Moses could not go into the Promised Land. Aaron, such a high priest, as evolved as he was, he made the golden calf. He himself threw the jewelry in the fire, and out popped the golden calf. Joseph knew his brothers were already angry and jealous of him, yet he told them of his dream where "you will all bow down to me." And they threw him in the pit for it.

Many listeners love the stories here, because it shows the people are real. The teachings are more like ideas. Perhaps our mind grasps the ideas, yet part of us feels, "I could never be that good." When we hear about real people with real flaws, we feel they are not so far removed from us.

Question: Can you say more about how our individual being belongs to our larger Self?

Your Larger Self is a collective of many beings, many souls who are sent here, each with their own Nefesh, Ruach, and Neshama (the levels of each soul). In that sense you are many. Your Larger Self is many. It sends down new beings all the time. You may perhaps recognize other souls as part of your group.

Yet you, as an individual, with your Nefesh (physical), Ruach (astral), and Neshama (mental/causal) - you also continue as the person you know yourself to be. When you drop your Nefesh, your physical body, then you move into your Ruach, the astral realm. In that realm emotions are primary, and you learn to deal with emotions. You learn better control of emotions. It's also the realm of speaking and sound.

Every level of your soul is meant to do its own learning before returning to your Larger Self.

Question: When you talk about these roots and branches of our soul groups, is it more like a forest?

Yes it is a forest. It is many big trees. It's the Garden of Eden.

You need to know that your Larger Self looks upon you with so much love. In a way, the deepest love we can find is between our self and our Larger Self. At the time of death, the Larger Self comes to embrace you and take you Home. It really can be a moment of deep love. That's what it is.

The Larger Self embraces you and says, "I love you so much, and I can't stay here long. Come with me. Come Home with me."

Question: If we need to find our direction, is it helpful to consult a psychic?

It depends on which floor of the building you're on. On the higher levels, there are no psychics available with that kind of sight. Even on the lower floors, when you drop into confusion and you want to find someone to advise you, there are messages offered all around you. Someone walks by on the sidewalk and you hear them say something that hits you just right.

When you need to find your way, Divine messages will pop up all around you. Tune in and listen.

Question: Please speak about how these ideas mesh with self-esteem?

Eventually happiness replaces self-esteem. You will reach an understanding where the issues of self-esteem simply don't matter anymore. Your happiness becomes so great that you are no longer speaking that language or thinking about it. Not to say self-esteem is not important. It is important. It's just that, the further you go on this path, that focus falls away while sheer happiness increases.

75 Hanukkah/ Chochmah, Wisdom

When God creates worlds, He uses Chochmah, which means wisdom. Not the wisdom we think of as being smart or wise. Rather, Chochmah is the very ocean of life force in all the worlds. Everything in every world draws life from Chochmah.

Chochmah is hidden, yet it's right here everywhere.

When the attribute of Chochmah, Wisdom, is awakened in a person, there is such an infusion of life force, it is as if the person gets their first taste of life itself. Before this they were living along, managing okay. When Wisdom is concealed you draw only a drop of it at a time, and you get along. Yet when you receive the gift of Wisdom, it's like your first taste of real life. When true Wisdom dawns, a person is absolutely filled with life.

In the Torah olive oil represents Wisdom. Wherever you read "olive oil" you may substitute "Wisdom" (life force) for the deeper meaning of the stories.

As we know, the story of Hanukkah tells us there was only enough oil to burn for one day in the Temple. The Maccabees had been attacked by an army of forty thousand, yet three hundred priests managed to win the war. They reclaimed the Temple in Jerusalem and prepared to rededicate it, lighting the Menorah once again. They found only one small cruse of oil still sealed and stamped by the high priest. Yet this oil lasted eight days, a miracle celebrated ever after.

So for the eight days of Hanukkah we increase the candles, increase the oil, every day. Or you could say we are becoming more alive with wisdom each passing day.

It's a miracle that we humans can be filled with wisdom as if we've never tasted life before. Here it is. Taste it.

You know how a key has little prongs, little bumps on it, to help it work? Well, there are two prongs on the key to the reservoir of Wisdom. When you have activated these two beliefs, then Wisdom will be drawn to you.

Before God there is no good or evil. All is good. Or, as we often say, "Gam zu l' tovah" - "This too is for the good."

Even what seems bad and difficult in our lives ultimately leads to good in some way. The ability to hold this belief is based on faith, not on fact. It takes faith to "see" the wisdom that is hidden from us. As King David said, "Taste and see that God is good."

The other key belief: all events happen by Divine providence. Nothing is random. If we call something a random event, it only means we haven't the wisdom and the broad perspective to see the hand of the Divine in it.

When we fully understand this precept, we know that nothing is wrong. Nothing is ever wrong.

If you adopt these double-prong beliefs, the next thing is, you will uncover your own collection of complaints, anger, vengeance, grief. You will see all the places in your life where

"I don't believe there was any participation of God in this." You will have lots of material to work through.

Eventually the double-prong approach changes the way you see the world. Things you used to get angry about don't touch you with anger anymore.

Olive oil - Chochmah - pours down, anointing the practitioners of these two understandings. Chochmah anoints you the same way kings were anointed with oil, because they needed wisdom to lead the nation. When you are anointed with Chochmah, you begin to ascend past the laws of Nature.

Without Chochmah, we see the laws of Nature at work. That is, cause and effect. We see the cause, so we can predict the effect. This is self-evident and self-repeating. We can prove it. No surprises.

But this perspective is only because Chochmah - the lights of Hanukkah - are not shining in the person.

Wisdom, when it pours upon us like olive oil, shows us first-hand that prayer is real. Prayer is real connection. In fact the word for prayer, "t'feela," means connection.

Oil, Chochmah, pours down and makes radical shifts from darkness to light. Miraculous things happen. Unexpected gifts drop into our lives, outside of regular cause and effect, outside the laws of Nature. Just like the way three hundred priests held off a whole army.

Almost more than the historical miracle, Hanukkah shows us the Hope we can have. This hope is worthy of celebration.

When we care for each other, as we do here, with no expectations, Hope is rekindled.

76 Paradox/ Your Large Soul View/ Karma/ Kindness

Question: We know that our mind makes form, according to our perceptions and vibrations. We know, as you've said, God is causing us to blossom in the beam of His attention and is pouring through us, making everything happen. At the same time, everything is already Created. We are told that everything that will ever exist is already Created by God. Help us understand how both of these are true?

Isaac answered by holding his hands in front of his face, with only a tiny gap to allow him to see one person at a time. "What can I see now, with a narrowed view? Only you, and now only the next person."

It's like a long storybook that is already written, but we can read only one page at a time. We are here now. We experience only one page now. But the whole book is written. We can't see the whole thing at once.

Imagine your Large Soul sending you out, lifetime after lifetime. It sends part of you to the causal plane and part to the astral plane, and sends you here to the physical. It's really not as defined as this, but for the sake of understanding we can work with it in this way.

The Large Soul may send parts only into the causal and/or astral. But if it goes all the way into the physical, it has the causal and astral layers for sure. It's like the root we spoke about, going deeper into the physical.

If you are here in the physical body, you know you also have counterparts in the causal and astral realms.

The Soul incarnates in order to learn and develop more skill in areas where it may be weak. For instance, your Large Soul may want to work on its skill of how to handle anger. Perhaps in past lifetimes you handled anger in a coarse way. Your anger was easily triggered and seeking vengeance. Perhaps part of you felt regret in that, and now the Large Soul wants to try again this lifetime to really focus and learn about anger.

So here you are, in a potentially angry moment. (He held his palms open, both sides balancing like a set of scales.)

Inside you hear a whisper: "I can't stand this - it isn't fair."

Another whisper arises and says, "Wait, not now. Speak of it later, but not now. Cool off."

But the situation is so heightened that the scales could tip in either direction. It's up to you to make your move and learn from it. It's your own learning. The Universe doesn't judge you.

If you manage to go with the more peaceful suggestion, then you experience patience - perhaps for the first time ever.

Now you have made one inroad into the experience of Patience. You feel its vibration. Now you will know how to get back here again, to Patience. You have a platform on which to build. Your Large Soul gains growth from this experience.

You are living page by page, and yes the whole book is already written. Although you feel you are making choices, the long view says it's all God doing this. It's not you doing anything at all. You are guided in everything, the good and the bad.

In fact there is nothing bad. It's all from God. All of it is good. There is no such thing as evil, when you see it from broad perspective. Yes there is suffering, there is difficulty, and all of that is valid. That is also true.

A person could take this teaching and say, "Well, whatever happens is meant to happen, so I don't have to try." But that's not the attitude we want. Don't stop efforting just because you know the whole book is already written.

The Sages looked for two things in their students:

First, the humility of not knowing the whole picture and not attempting to control it.

Second, a willingness to put forth effort. In fact if students assumed a controlling attitude or believed they could control God's gifts to them, the teacher would give them assignments that brought them low.

Anyone may be brought low on any given day. Always for a purpose. Have the humility to know you are not in control of anything.

When your life is done, your body falls away, yet your consciousness is still living in the astral and causal planes. You have more to learn on those planes before returning fully to your Large Soul.

Question: Would part of yourself or part of your vibration still remain here on earth after you die?

It remains in the consciousness of others.

Most of us will have further lessons to work on slowly in the astral and causal planes. Sometimes an elevated soul who completes their work here in the physical goes straight back through those upper planes in one jump, returning to the Large Soul. But that's exceptional.

Now the residues of your elevated vibration assists your "soul group" even after you die. Your vibration remains in the consciousness of others. People remember the kindness of an ordinary person. Perhaps you did nothing "important" in your life, yet people will say of you, "He stopped and helped me change my tire. I will never forget his or her kindness, just the way they lived in the world."

Question: Where does karma fit into all this?

Karma is about fairness. Karma keeps track of your debts so you don't have to. Everything you inflict upon others is naturally inflicted upon you, at some point later. So you gain empathy for everyone's suffering.

Our debt is really so immense we can't possibly pay it all at once. The Soul may take a span of two hundred lives to repay everything, on the installment plan.

When you are all paid up, Justice becomes kind. Justice is not only about negatives, about paying what you owe. It's also about receiving the good from the seeds you have sown.

Our Teachers celebrate the kindness in an ordinary life. Even one mitzvah, one good deed, makes life worthwhile. The Sages say even one moment may be the reason you incarnated. One moment could be the fulfillment of your whole life. It doesn't matter that you have no achievements, that you're not known for anything, that you didn't accomplish anything big. Your kindness is what matters.

Consider one good man, like Mr. Wong, on a dock somewhere in China, fishing today. He is just another inconsequential man, one among millions. We might even say he doesn't matter. His life is not important to any important people.

Yet he loves his wife and children. He brings home a fish for them simply because they are hungry. This is how he shows his love, by protecting and providing for them. It's just a fish. But his intent - his love - is so much more than just a fish.

His mitzvah is a bright point of light that returns to his Large Soul. That bright point remains there forever, because it is love. It is eternal.

77 Expansion, Evaporation Is True Prayer/ Gratitude

Isaac began by reading a story about Sri Yukteswar (1855-1936) from Yogananda's Autobiography of a Yogi.

In Sri Yukteswar's youth, when Yukteswar was very ill and thin, his teacher, Lahiri Mahasaya, sort of teased him into wellness. First Lahiri implied that he might be better the next day. When Yukteswar was so, he praised his teacher, thinking Lahiri had healed him.

But Lahiri said Yukteswar had invigorated himself. Yukteswar complained about how long he'd been sick, and Lahiri replied that yes, it was tough, maybe the next days wouldn't go so well. They didn't.

Finally Lahiri made him understand how his belief was being fulfilled every day. His thoughts directly impacted his condition. When Yukteswar fully understood this, Lahiri told him he could be well immediately through his thought/belief.

Lahiri looked deep into his eyes, and within one second, Yukteswar gained back the fifty pounds he had lost during this long illness. When his mother and friends saw him, they were amazed at the change. He kept that weight on evermore. It wasn't a trick.

Thus we see how strong our thoughts are, how our belief brings our reality to us. Like Yukteswar, if we believe we are sick, we are. If we believe in our own wellness, it comes to us.

Any experience we have, especially if it repeats itself, we call it truth and we believe in it. Its form becomes more and more solid to us. The belief becomes more difficult to change. After all, our life seems to be working that way. It's true. It's something that keeps happening to us. We feel we can depend on this part of our truth, our reality. And yet, it is our own thought which keeps that form in place. If we could change our thought, the form would also change.

Everything created is composed of vibration. All sorts of vibration.

I look at your beautiful face, and that is one way of seeing it, the vibration of your skin, for instance. An X-ray (gamma rays) of your face would look entirely different.

If we had full sight, we would be able to see every vibration. We would see the bones deep within. The blood vessels would be a different vibration. The muscles, the skin, each has its unique vibration. We would see all these layers. We would also see the vibration of energies inside and around us, a rainbow of colors in our aura.

We would see the vibration of the chair underneath us. We would see the way our vibrations blend into the chair's vibrations. We would see our vibrations blending into our neighbor's vibrations. This is happening even though we can't see it.

There are no boundaries. No boundaries between us nor between anything.

We would understand how the world of vibration is really an ocean, always flowing and changing. Everything is shared, without boundaries.

But in our dense awareness we can't see all that. We have to look for other ways to experience it.

The Sages tell us rain is the way heaven connects to earth. How does earth connect to heaven? Through evaporation. Water evaporates in an invisible way. Nobody notices it, as water changes into vapor and goes up into the clouds. The clouds have to be filled with moisture before they can rain down on us. To evaporate, the water has to lose its form and become like mist before it can be taken up into the clouds.

Good prayer is evaporation.

When we can lose our form, lose our thought, and dissolve ourselves in prayer or meditation, then evaporation happens.

We let go of form when we go to that place where nothing is wrong.

We put everything else aside and engage in real prayer, real meditation. That's when we evaporate. This is the way to connect to heaven and seed the clouds.

When a person holds onto their lack and pleads with God to change that lack, whether it's an issue of money or relationships or spirituality - when they keep that lack in their mind, they hold onto their current form. They say, "God, I'm so tired of this situation, I hate it, please change it for me." This person is voicing fatigue, hate, helplessness, deficiency.

They are not evaporating, not dissolving. They aren't sending any water up to the clouds to build into rain. This kind of prayer, spoken from a constricted lacking vibration, often doesn't work at all. It is more of the same lack. It perpetuates the existing form.

What do you need in order to evaporate? You need heat. That heat is gratitude.

Look at whatever is truly working in your life, even if it's only one small wonderful thing. Your gratitude for that enables you to reach evaporation. Your gratitude and full focus on such things allows you to dissolve and evaporate enough so you loosen your grip on the old pattern, the form you'd like to change.

Have you ever met someone who is simply happy with whatever comes their way? It seems the happier they get, the more blessings come into their lives?

You look at them and say, "It's not fair!" But they have learned to evaporate. They have learned to appreciate, even when at first there was little to appreciate. They dwell in such gratitude. Blessings rain upon them all the time. They have let go of the forms that restricted them. They did it through gratitude.

So expansion and evaporation is true prayer. And the root of prayer is gratitude.

You may also have friends or relatives who drag you into supporting their unwanted forms. They complain about some aspect of their lives, and perhaps you may see how they perpetuate it by constantly keeping it alive. It's the truth, after all. It's reality. But underneath that, it's a form kept alive by their thoughts and their focus upon it.

But you're a friend, and when they come to you with their troubles, you may feel obligated to support their view. You agree with them. You commiserate. You help them keep that form going.

If you really want to be a good friend, you will refuse to buy into their sad story. You can listen with understanding but at the same time not feed their story. Don't take it on as your own reality. Feel within yourself that it is not true. Don't believe it. Whatever it is, it's just another changeable form.

What they really want is for people to buy into their story. That supports them and feeds the form. The more people who buy into it, the more solid the form becomes. But you don't have to buy into their story. Carry an attitude that says, okay, there's your story, but I don't really believe in it. The sun is still shining. Your attitude or even your words may give them a hint that maybe their story isn't as real as they thought.

So you learn true prayer. You practice gratitude. You learn to dissolve and expand and evaporate regularly, to send water up to the heavens, up to the clouds.

But this issue you want to change, this stuck form, is still there.

You're impatient. You want it to change right now. What does that do to you? It constricts you back into the densest form again. You say "right now" and you just imposed limitation and constriction and lack. You want it; you don't have it yet. You're standing in deficiency.

Go to expansion, to a place where you feel so comfortable and so full that you forget about any deficiency.

Let's say you're hiking along on a beautiful day. Your consciousness is so expanded. Your awareness is in the sunshine, the mountain, the flowers, the birds. You are so expanded. Where's your body? You forgot about it. You feel fine. You're not thinking about your body. Suddenly you stub your toe. Ouch. Immediately your consciousness zooms down and in. It concentrates everything into that toe. Your entire being is now in one toe.

You're in pain. You might yell or say a few choice words, stop and hold your toe, rub it.

What happens next? Do you have to say a mantra or something to return to the beauty of the day? Not usually. You simply turn your attention back to the flowers and the trees, and soon the pain in your toe is gone again. This tells us that the Universe is set up to encourage our expansion, our evaporation. We want to expand. We are meant to evaporate.

We don't have to keep our consciousness focused on something painful. When we do, it's by choice and by habit and by belief that this form is true. Pain creates form easily. Form arises easier from pain than from anything else in the human mind.

Yet we don't have to invest in our pain. We perpetuate it by our attention to it.

How would you make this work in your own life?

Through daily meditation and prayer. Learn to evaporate every day. This practice brings it into being in your life. The more often you evaporate, the easier it comes when you need it.

This week in the Torah, the viceroy Joseph had not yet revealed himself, but told his brothers they must leave their youngest brother Benjamin with him in Egypt. Judah, Yehudah, pleaded with Joseph and offered himself as a servant instead. He said the loss of Benjamin would kill their father. Then Joseph wept and revealed that he was their brother.

Our Teachers say that Joseph "rains" down upon Yehudah, in response to Yehudah's gratitude for all the grain, the money and generosity Joseph had given them. Yehudah represents the earth and Joseph the heavens. Yehudah evaporates and humbles himself. Joseph showers blessings upon him.

This is also symbolized in the sefirot of Malkhut going up to Yesod, and Yesod showering down upon Malkhut.

Shabbos is a time when there is no lack. It's the day we should wear our best clothes and enjoy the best food. We rest from all our troubles. There are no troubles on this day of the week.

This puts us into a place of expansiveness, evaporation, connection.

This puts us into true prayer.

True gratitude.

Appendix   Tree of Life, Sefirot

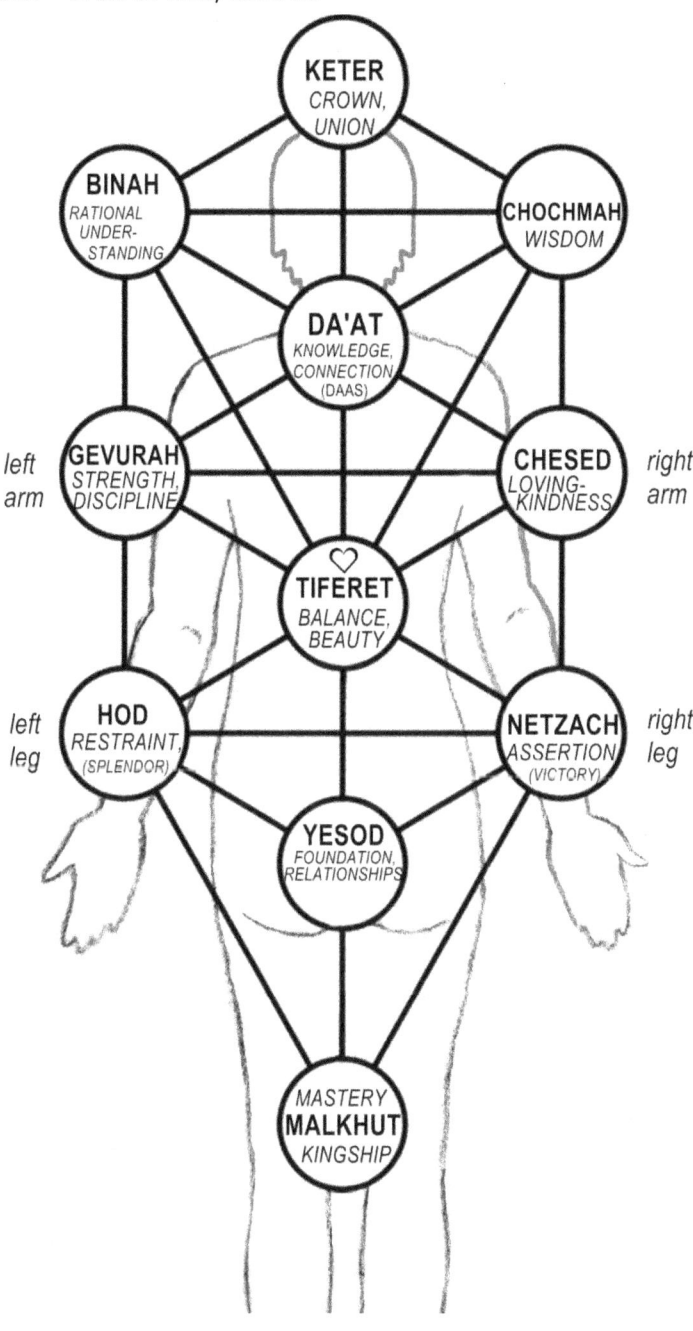

Four Worlds

Keeping in mind an infinite number of worlds -
the Four Worlds are also seen as levels of consciousness.

Atzilut
world of emanation
formless, expansive, blissful
Chaya level of soul

Beriah
world of creation, intellect, causal plane
Neshama level of soul

Yetzirah
world of formation, emotion, astral plane
Ruach level of soul

Assiyah
physical world of action and density
Nefesh level of soul

Encapsulations of Many of Isaac's Teachings

(Courtesy of his First Scribe)

Gam Zoo L'-to-va ~ This, too, is for the good.
Give Loving Attention.
Let It Go.
Transmute the Will to Receive into the Desire to Bestow.
Let Kindness be the Guide.

My Child, see my hand reaching to you
back through time
With the love you needed then
but could not find.
Try to take hold of it now
and understand
That our future depends upon
our joining hands.

Spiritually speaking, being "100% Natural" is not complimentary. Go beyond the animal nature and become super-natural.

Take the High Road.

If you believe
that things can be broken,
Then believe
that they can be repaired.
(from Rebbe Nachman of Breslov)

Find Contentment in the Perfection of This Moment.
Trust that Cosmic Justice will Take Care of all Injustices.
Enjoy Life in Moderation.
Uplift Desires and Fears into Love and Awe for G-d.

Raising voices, closing ears,
Anger tears apart.
But where there is love,
a whisper will do
to open minds and hearts.

Calm the Mind.
Balance Divine Providence with Human Effort.
Truth = the Facts, Moderated by Kindness
Live a Life of Balance.
Be a Pipeline for Blessing.
Stop and Think: Is this the Right Time to Say That?
Learn to Say "No" Gently.
Return Home.
The World Is a Mirror. It reflects what we bring before it. To see more Loving Kindness in the world, be more loving and kinder.

In the Theater of the World, there must be enough darkness for the "Movie of Life" to be seen.

Divine Providence is Always with us, Caring, Guiding and Helping.

Some eyes are seeking only to heal
fitting pieces together again,
Holding a vision of the way things could be
and applying love's glue to mend.

Purity of Thought, Speech and Action
We Misidentify with the Body-Mind.
Be Mobile in the Multi-storied Building of Consciousness.
Reawaken Childlike Wonder.
Re-contextualize Problems: De-focus on them by seeing them in the context of the rest of life.

The Lessons of Manna: We receive what we need from Above. One's job is a vessel through which needs may be met. Treat your job with respect.

Humility is the Crowning Virtue.
It is a Great Thing, a Holy Highway, to be in Joy, Always Be in Joy. (from Rebbe Nachman of Breslov)

Live Comfortably among Those with Different Points of View.

Index - Glossary

Abraham 120, 159, 189, 239, 249-250
Adam 108-109
Ahavah (Love) 81, 100, 105
Amalek (doubt/enemy of Moses) 38, 53, 228-229
astral plane 59, 116, 178, 202, 206-207, 222, 251, 257-9
Atzilut (world of emanation, highest realm) 224, 225, 272
Baal Shem Tov (founded Hasidism) . 13, 36, **46**, 139, 148, 193
Baba Sali (Sephardic Rabbi, kabbalist) 43, 124, 133, 165
Chesed (loving-kindness) 21-22, 239, 250
Chochmah (wisdom) 15, 80, 224-226, 253, 255
Gevurah (discipline) ... 21-22, 72, 120, 130-132, 191, 219, 239
Havayah (Eternal Being) 19, 84-85, 145, 206
Keter (Crown, Union) 20-21, 80, 190, 242
mitzvah (good deed) 26, 59, 60, 259-260
Moses 19, 20, 38, 71, 176, 177, 229, 250
Nefesh (bodily soul) 33, 41, 59, 206, 251, 272
Neshama (higher soul) 41, 84-86, 112, 180, 206, 235, 251
Passover (liberation from slavery) 185, 191
Purim holiday 25, 124, 167-169
Rabbi Nachman 33, 147, 192, 212, 274, 275
relationships 12-13
Ribnitzer Rebbe **56**, 57, 61-62, 107-108
sefirot (divine attributes) 21, 80, 144, 166, 267, **271**
Sh'ma (daily prayer, Listen: God is One) 37, 80, 104, 235

Shekhinah (Divine Presence) 13, 73, 227
Sukkot (joyful autumn holiday) 104-106, 107, 227-229
Talmud (Jewish law and legend).................... 36, 159, **180**, 193
Tiferet (Balance, Beauty) 21, 121, 144-145, 239-242
Tree of Life (path to God/ divine attributes)........................ 271
tzaddik (saint) 37, 56, 61, 117, 125, 126, 177
Yogananda (taught Kriya Yoga) .. **101**, 183-184, 194, 197, 261
Yukteswar (guru teacher of Yogananda) 194, **261**
Zusya (Rabbi Zusya).. 22, 40, 164

Acknowledgements

Deep Thanks to Isaac for sharing so much with all of us, these decades.

Deep Thanks to our awesome spiritual community - you know who you are.

Deep Thanks to each and every friend who encouraged this book into being.

Peace to you whose eyes fall upon these pages. Thanks for choosing them.

About the Author

Born from a lineage of spiritual human beings, Diane Langlois Stallings spent fourteen years learning and growing with this Rebbe and Community. This book is written through her filters, and cannot convey the totality of the original spontaneous oral teachings.

Diane and her husband have walked the Quarters of Jerusalem and the Temples of India. They raised two wonderful young people.

Glad to teach meditation and energy enrichment in Phoenix and Fountain Hills, Arizona, Diane also enjoys writing on health, energy medicine, self-care, spirit, and inspiration at joystreamhealth.wordpress.com.

To stay in touch with this book series go to walkingthebridgewisdom.wordpress.com.

"Diane possesses the unique gift of "the scribe" of old, who often committed to memory what was said by the Rabbi on Shabbat, when it was not permitted to use pen and paper, and wrote the words later from memory. We are gifted indeed by her beautiful words and heart." - RLN

www.ingramcontent.com/pod-product-compliance
Lightning Source LLC
Chambersburg PA
CBHW061426040426
42450CB00007B/915